New York Beauty Quilts
ELECTRIFIED
By Linda J. Hahn and Deborah G. Stanley

New York Beauty Quilts
ELECTRIFIED
By Linda J. Hahn and Deborah G. Stanley

Landauer Publishing *(www.landauerpub.com)* is an imprint of
Fox Chapel Publishing Company, Inc.

Copyright © 2019 by Linda J. Hahn, Deborah G. Stanley and
Fox Chapel Publishing Company, Inc., 903 Square Street, Mount Joy, PA 17552.

Project Team:
Vice President–Content: Christopher Reggio
Editors: Laurel Albright/Sue Voegtlin
Copy Editor: Laura Taylor
Designer: Laurel Albright
Photographer: Sue Voegtlin

ISBN: 978-1-947163-15-7

Library of Congress Cataloging-in-Publication Data

Names: Hahn, Linda, author. | Stanley, Deborah G., author.
Title: New York beauty quilts electrified / Linda J. Hahn and Deborah G.
  Stanley.
Description: Mount Joy, PA : Landauer Publishing, [2019]
Identifiers: LCCN 2019008565 | ISBN 9781947163157 (pbk.)
Subjects: LCSH: Patchwork--Patterns. | Quilting--Patterns. | New York beauty
  quilts.
Classification: LCC TT835 .H2578 2019 | DDC 746.46/041--dc23
LC record available at https://lccn.loc.gov/2019008565

We are always looking for talented authors. To submit an idea, please send a brief inquiry to
acquisitions@foxchapelpublishing.com.

Printed in Singapore

21 20 19   2 4 6 8 10 9 7 5 3 1

This book has been published with the intent to provide accurate and authoritative information in
regard to the subject matter within. While every precaution has been taken in the preparation of this
book, the author and publisher expressly disclaim any responsibility for any errors, omissions, or
adverse effects arising from the use or application of the information contained herein.

Table of Contents

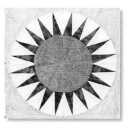

Introduction

When I heard Linda Hahn would be writing her next New York Beauty book with her dear friend, Deborah Stanley, I was excited. *New York Beauty Quilts Electrified* is the third New York Beauty book from Linda, and like the other two books it explores creative designs incorporating the traditional block pattern. In this book, Linda and Deborah showcase the versatility of the basic New York Beauty block by using it in new ways.

Our love of New York Beauties is what we share in common. A few years ago I wrote a book covering the history of the pattern—*New York Beauty, Quilts from the Volckening Collection*—and the last quilt in the book was a design called "Bensonhurst Blooms" from Linda's *New York Beauty Diversified* book.

The creative use of blocks as pictorial elements represented the last word in New York Beauties, but there was much more to the story.

New York Beauty quilts first appeared in the middle nineteenth century, when the burgeoning American textile industry gave quilt makers the freedom to explore complex, geometric patchwork designs using a surplus of new fabric.

The radiant sunburst motif was not known as New York Beauty at first. Before newspapers and magazines started publishing and naming patterns around the turn of the twentieth century, quilt block patterns did not really have standardized names at all.

"New York Beauty" was the name of a pattern introduced by Mountain Mist in 1930. The company included patterns as a premium, to promote the sales of rolls of quilt batting. Unfortunately, the designers took creative license with the historical account about the inspiration quilt, saying the pattern originated in 1776. It may have seemed plausible at the time, but today we know it was not true.

Throughout history, New York Beauty quilts shared specific visual elements in common, such as technically challenging curved seams and sharp points. Originally these elements were hand pieced without foundation, and that's the way it was for roughly 150 years.

In the late 1980s and early 1990s, several artists began successful experimentation with paper foundation piecing for the New York Beauty and other complex patterns. That's when the motif started to significantly evolve. Artists introduced bold new fabrics and colors, created innovative designs and gave new life to the traditional block pattern.

A hundred years from today people will glance back at the explosively creative period of quilt making in the late 20th and early 21st centuries and they will look at this book, *New York Beauty Quilts Electrified* and see the most innovative quilt makers of our time having lots of fun with colorful, imaginative quilts.

Bill Volckening

Author of *New York Beauty, Quilts from the Volckening Collection*

Award-winning blog *Wonkyworld*: **collecting quilts from the perspective of a 21st-century collector**

Definitions

Before you begin, please read through the following definitions of the various terms and abbreviations that we will be using throughout this book.

WOF: Width of Fabric—selvage to selvage—usually 40" to 42" (101.6 to 106.68cm) of usable fabric

HST: half-square triangle

RST: right sides of the fabrics together

RSU: right side of fabric up

RSD: right side of fabric down

Connector: small square of fabric sewn on the diagonal to create a triangle shape on a larger square or rectangle (sometimes referred to as a "stitch and flip" corner)

Arc Foundation: the "paper" part of the New York Beauty block

Spire: the "points" in the New York Beauty block arc foundation

Background Spire: the larger "points" in the New York Beauty block arc foundation

Pie: the pie-shaped section of the New York Beauty block

Background: the top of the New York Beauty block

Cutaway: the piece of fabric that you cut out from behind the spires as you piece the arc foundation. Use these pieces for mini New York Beauties.

General Hints

Stitch Length

If you are using regular copy paper or vellum for your project, you will need to shorten your stitch length. You don't want to shorten it so much that if you end up having to rip out stitches, you also rip the fabric. If you are using the recommended foundation paper, there is no need to worry about shortening the stitches since you won't be removing the paper. You can use the default stitch on your machine.

The Piecing Factor

Everyone has their own personal preferences and thoughts when it comes to piecing. One person may choose to rip out a seam several times to get it perfect while others are quite content if their piecing is "off" by a thread or two. We understand and respect each person's choice and all those in between!

Chain Piecing

We recommend making one block to learn the technique. Once you understand and are comfortable with the way we foundation piece, you will (if you are comfortable doing so) be able to chain piece the arc foundations. We usually work on four to six blocks at a time.

Quilt Yardage

Many of the quilts in this book offer you the opportunity to incorporate your own interpretation and design elements into them. The instructions we provide for each quilt are what we used for the quilt design shown. That said, we have also built in some extra yardage into the fabric requirements to allow you to have a little extra in the event that you wish to incorporate your own design elements. Backing fabric yardage provided assumes that you will be piecing

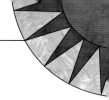

the back together with a vertical seam. Binding fabric yardage provided is calculated for 2½" (6.35cm) wide binding strips.

Starching

Whether or not to starch your fabrics is a personal preference. We like to heavily starch our fabrics. Think…"Starched is good…Crispy is better!" This is especially true for the pie shape since the starch will help keep any stretching or distortion under control. Our starch of preference is Niagara Spray Starch in a pump bottle, but others will also work.

Rulers and Cutters

We have found that the 9½" (24.13cm) Omnigrid® ruler works great. In fact, the only rulers we use are the 6" x 24" (15.24 x 60.96cm) ruler for strips, and the 9½" (24.13cm) square for everything else! It fits your hand so there is minimal slippage, and can fit in your purse. When cutting multiple layers, we like to use a 45mm cutter. You can grip it better to apply enough pressure to make a nice clean cut. Change your blade if you find your cuts are not going through all the layers of fabric.

Templates for Pie and Background Shapes

You can either make your own or you can purchase a kit that contains reusable foundation piecing stencils, and custom-made acrylic templates. If you are making your own templates, use heavy weight template plastic. See page 18 for instructions on Preparing the Pie and Background Shapes.

Foundation Paper

There are many different types of foundation paper on the market, and you are welcome to use the paper of your choice. Our paper of preference, of course, is our foundation paper, available at www.*froghollowdesigns. com*. We like it because it can be left in the quilt and that means no more ripping out the paper.

Frog Hollow Designs foundation paper will soften up over time, and will become a thin layer of polyester inside the quilt if washed. It can also go through your printer.

If you choose another type of foundation paper, we recommend using a Vellum or translucent foundation paper. The translucent paper is what makes this technique so easy, rather than the standard printer paper.

If you are using foundation paper that must be removed, do not remove it until you have sewn the block into the quilt. To remove, you can spritz the area with water to soften up the paper to make it easier to remove.

Copier Distortion

It happens…all copiers are not created equal. Before you copy your entire package of foundation paper, make one copy of the pattern and check the measurements. This applies not just to this pattern, but to every foundation pattern that you may use. If you copy something at home, and then go into work to use the work copier, you may find that the copies are not the same size. Try to copy all the patterns on the same copier for consistency.

Scanning

Pay attention if you choose this option. Make sure that when you print the pattern, you are printing actual size and not "fit to page."

Alternative to Copying

You may wish to consider the New York Beauty Quilt kit available on our website that contains a laser-cut, reusable foundation stencil. Trace the pattern onto the foundation paper using a Pigma pen.

Choosing Fabrics

Choosing fabric for a quilt is a personal choice. You may be choosing for a specific decor of a room, or perhaps the favorite colors of the recipient. To give you an idea of how we choose fabrics, we will use the fabrics that we chose for the step-out samples.

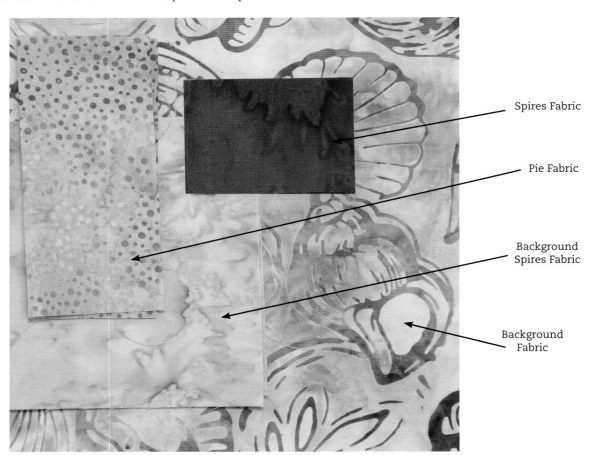

Spires Fabric

Pie Fabric

Background Spires Fabric

Background Fabric

Linda found this seashell batik print that she really loved (now that she lives in Florida). Since the background piece of the block is the most visible, we decided to use this fabric as the focus fabric.

The teal solid is for the background spires since we wanted those to blend into the background to make the spires more prominent.

We chose the berry solid for the spires as it is a color pulled from the seashell print.

The small dotted pink print is for the pie and has some of the colors from the seashell print.

Directional fabric, stripes or large prints, do not work well for this technique. These fabrics can be incorporated into the sashing or borders.

The New York Beauty Block

Originally referred to as the Crown of Thorns, the New York Beauty moniker comes from the similarity of the Statue of Liberty crown. The arc foundation in our blocks is part of what makes this block so attractive, but also a little scary to those making it for the first time. Our technique takes away the fear and complexity, and makes this a fun block for anyone with basic quilting skills.

Preparing the Arc Foundations

Making Copies
Refer to page 84, for templates, to make copies of the arc foundations. Two arc patterns will fit on one 8½" x 11" (21.59 x 27.94cm) sheet of foundation paper, if you are tracing from our stencil.

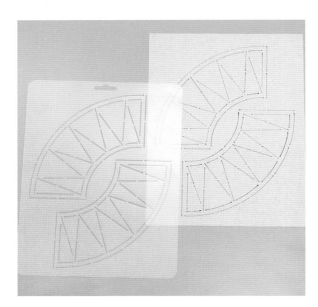

Cutting Out the Arc Foundations
Cut each arc foundation out leaving approximately ⅛" to ¼" (0.3176 to 0.64cm) around the outermost edges of the printed foundation. This is so you have something to sew off of and a little extra to "grab." You can cut out multiple arcs at a time by pinning the foundation paper sheets together.

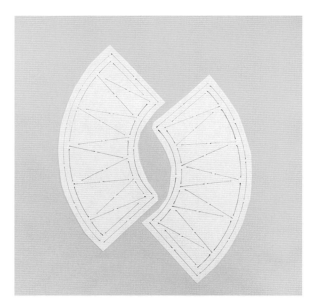

TIP

Before starting a project, it's a good idea to practice making an arc.

To follow this step-by-step, cut:

- (6) 3" x 4" (7.62 x 10.16cm) pieces for background spires

- (5) 2½" x 3½" (6.35 x 8.89cm) pieces for small spires

Note: These fabric measurements are used for all five-spire arc foundations in the projects.

Piecing the Arc Foundations

Strange as this may sound, we have found that students understand the process of piecing the arc foundation when we use their "belly" as a reference point. This is exactly how we teach the process in class.

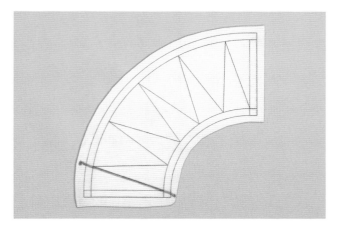

1. Place the arc foundation flat on the table in front of you. Looking down at the foundation, the first diagonal line (highlighted in blue) is the line you will begin piecing on.

2. As you piece the arc, always lay the foundation back down on the table. Place the 3" x 4" (7.62 x 10.16cm) background spire right side up. Hold at your belly and slide the piece over the first diagonal line approximately ¼" (0.64cm).

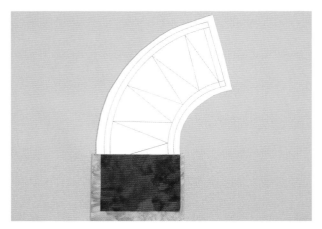

3. Place a 2½" x 3½" (6.35 x 8.89cm) spire piece right sides together, aligning the raw edges with the background spire. Try to keep the pieces centered between the outermost lines.

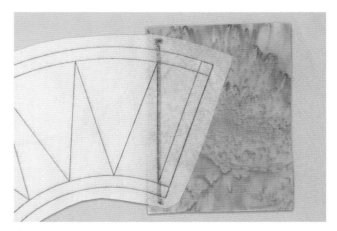

4. Flip the pieces over and sew from the outermost seam line at the top to the outermost seam line at the bottom. Sew all the way off the paper. This also facilitates chain piecing, if you choose to do that.

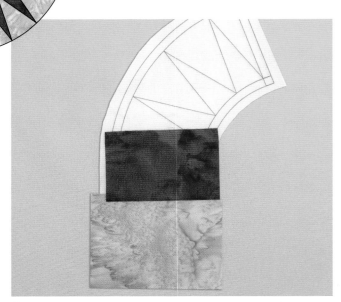

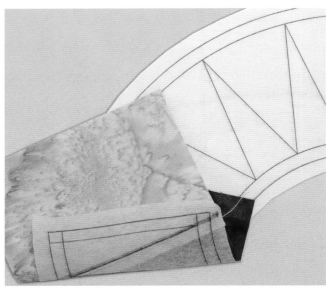

5. Flip the foundation over, open the seam and finger press.

6. With the foundation pointing toward the belly, fold the spire piece back to the next diagonal line and crease the seam with your finger or press lightly with an iron. This is the placement and sewing line for the next spire. Always fold the foundation away from you. If you fold it toward you, it will distort the fabric underneath and make an inaccurate placement line.

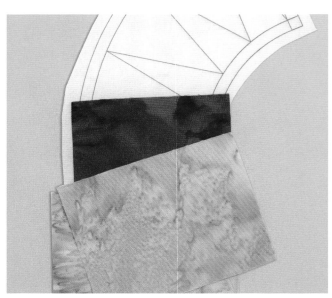

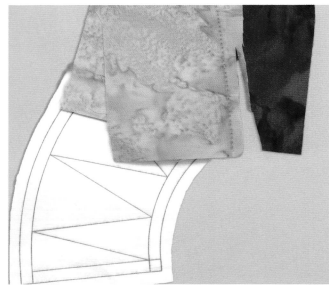

7. Place the next 3" x 4" (7.62 x 10.16cm) background spire, right sides together, approximately ¼" (0.64cm) over the creased line. Flip the piece to the back and sew on the creased line through the edge of the paper.

8. Fold the arc foundation out of the way and trim the excess fabric from underneath the spires with a rotary cutter or scissors, leaving an approximate ¼" (0.64cm) seam allowance. See page 24, Make a Mini!, to use up these cutaways for a miniature New York Beauty quilt.

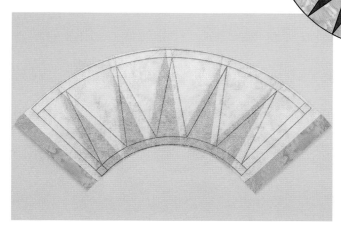

9. Continue rolling, creasing, sewing, and trimming the spire pieces all the way down the arc and press after each piece is sewn.

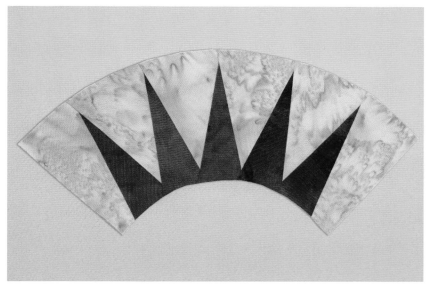

10. Turn the arc over and cut along the outer curved lines of the foundation. On the straight sides, leave an extra ¼" (0.64cm) to just under ½" (1.27cm). You will be able to adjust this allowance once you are familiar with the technique.

11. The arc foundation is trimmed before setting in the pie and the background pieces.

TIP

Add to the Straight...
Cut to the Curve

On the straight sides of the arc foundation, leave ¼" to ½" (0.64 to 1.27cm) of extra fabric. This will be trimmed away after the block is finished. When trimming the arc, "cut to the curve," which is the outermost line of the foundation.

Preparing the Pie and Background Shapes

The templates on page 86 are used to cut the pie and background shapes. You can make your own, tracing the templates onto template plastic.

You can purchase a set of acrylic templates on our website, www.*froghollowdesigns.com*.

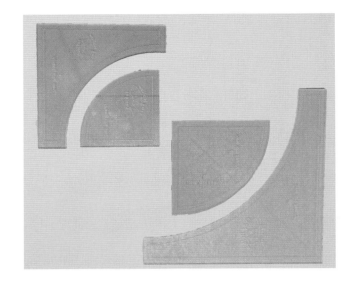

1. Make a paper copy of the templates on page 87. To make a set of templates, copy the background and pie templates onto a sheet of heavy template plastic. Glide a gluestick around the edges of the paper templates and place the template plastic on top. Smooth down the paper copy with your hands.

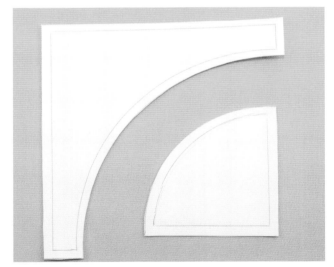

2. Use appropriate scissors to cut out the templates on the outside line. Don't worry about adding the inside seam line.

TIP

We recommend starching the 8" (20.32cm) and the 4½" (11.43cm) squares of fabric before cutting out the background pieces. It adds to the stability of the bias cut curves.

Add to the Straight...Cut to the Curve

Add to the straight...you will be adding approximately ¼" to ½" (0.64 to 1.27cm) to each straight edge of a shape. Cut to the curve...when cutting the curves, follow the template edge.

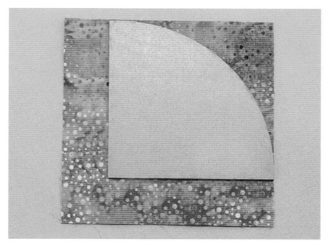

3. The pie shape is cut from a 4½" (11.43cm) square. You can bring the curved part of the template all the way up to the edge of the square. Trace around the template and leave extra fabric along the straight edges.

4. The background shape is cut from an 8" (20.32cm) square. Once again, trace around the template and leave extra fabric along the straight edges.

5. Leftover fabric from pie and background cuts can be put to good use. Think creatively. If you are making a scrap quilt, you can get several shapes from leftover pieces. We get most of our mini backgrounds and/or pies using up this fabric.

Piecing the Block Components

All of your block components are ready to be sewn into a block. All you need is ONE PIN. When you are ready to sew, use a regular presser foot, one without a flange. If your machine has a needle down feature, now is the time to use it. If not, hand crank the needle to the down position before repositioning the fabric pieces.

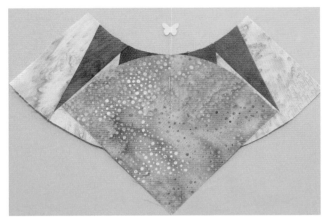

1. The pie shape is sewn in first. Fold the pie in half and crease the center at the curve. With right sides together, line up the crease with the bottom of the center spire of the arc foundation. Pin in place.

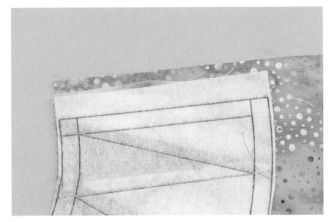

2. Pull the pie around and overlap the arc foundation approximately ¼" (0.64cm). You want a little extra pie fabric to extend over the edge of the arc foundation.

3. Take a few stitches to anchor the pieces and remove the pin. With the needle in the down position, pull the arc foundation to the left while gently pulling the pie to the right. Do not force the pieces together. Taking a few stitches before you reposition will alleviate puckers.

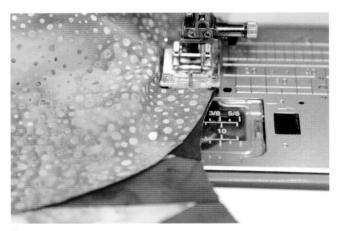

4. The pie is cut larger, so you have wiggle room to gently pull it over to the arc foundation. Try to keep the edge of the presser foot aligned with the edge of the arc foundation.

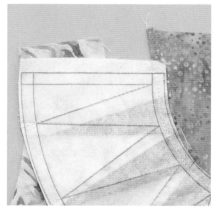

5. When you are finished sewing, don't press or do anything other than attach the next piece.

6. Fold the background piece in half and crease the curve. With right sides together, line up the crease with the top of the center spire, and pin in place.

7. Overlap the background piece approximately ¼" (0.64cm) to extend over the edge of the arc foundation.

8. The pin can stay in until the background begins to bunch up as the needle gets closer to the pin. Release the pin and continue, gently pulling the background fabric to the edge of the arc foundation.

9. When you are finished sewing, press the block in an up-and-down motion to avoid stretching the piece out of shape.

The Final Trim

It's time to trim up these blocks and make the magic happen! The key to all the blocks fitting together is consistency. This technique becomes faster with every block you trim.

1. Place the block, right side up, on a cutting mat, with spires pointing up and to the right, as shown.

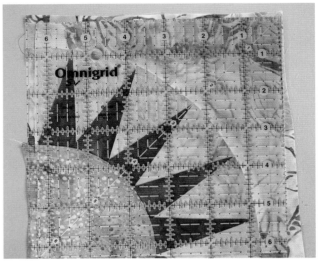

2. Place the number 1 of a 6½" (16.51cm) ruler on the top right corner of the block.

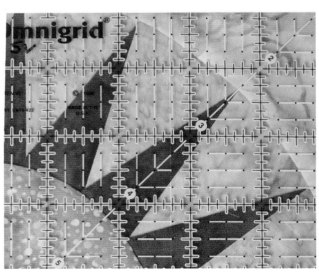

3. Place the diagonal line of the ruler centered through the center spire.

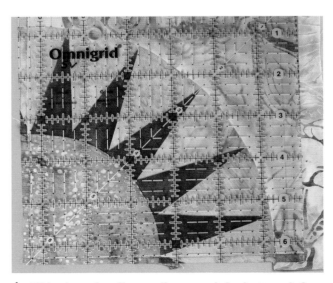

4. Slide the ruler diagonally toward the bottom left corner of the block, watching the 6" (15.24cm) line on both sides of the ruler.

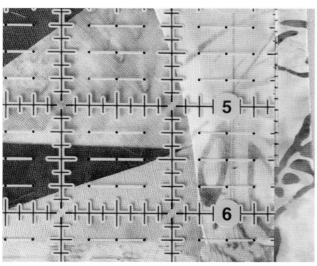

5. Stop when the ¾" (1.91cm) marks align on the seam lines of the arc and background. Trim the block on the top and right side of the ruler.

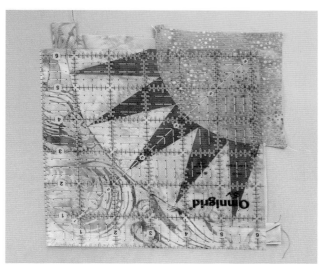

6. Turn the block 180° and realign the ruler along the bottom and left edge of the block.

7. Trim along the top and right side of the ruler.

8. The New York Beauty block now measures 6½" (16.51cm) square.

Using Split Background and Pie Shapes

You can easily add more design elements to your basic New York Beauty blocks by incorporating two color background or pie shapes. Adding these pieces takes a little more time to do and you need to be a little more accurate with your piecing.

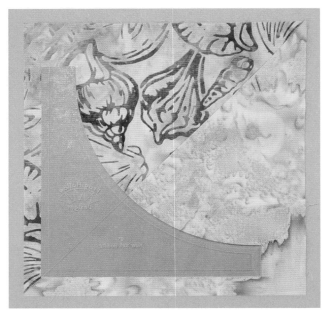

Adding a Split Background

1. Following the instructions for Alternate Blocks, on page 23, create a half-square triangle that is 8" (20.32cm).

2. Place the diagonal line of the template on the seam allowance. Add a very small amount to the straight edges and "cut to the curve."

3. Pin the background to the pieced arc. Sew with the background on top.

> **TIP**
>
> Using solid fabrics will show any misalignments more than if you use a print fabric.
>
> A generous amount of starch helps keep the pie and background pieces from getting distorted, especially if you have to unsew and reapply.

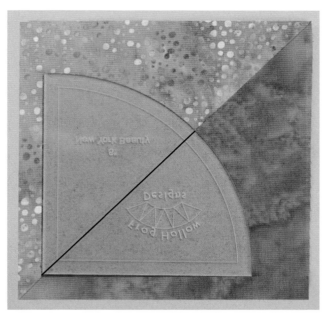

Adding a Split Pie

1. Following the instructions on page 23, create a half-square triangle that is 4" to 4½" (10.16 to 11.43cm). Either size will work.

2. Place the diagonal line of the template on the seam allowance. Add a very small amount to the straight edges and "cut to the curve."

3. Pin the pie in place with the pin pointed up and the tip coming up at about ½" (0.64cm) from the edge of the fabric. Sew with the pie on top of the arc.

4. When doing the final trim, the diagonal line of the ruler should be on the seam allowance of the pie shape.

Sewing the Blocks Together

If you have made four blocks, you can sew them together to make a beautiful New York Beauty full sun block. It's always exciting to see this finished block for the first time.

1. Align two blocks, right sides together. Pin from the inside out, coming up with the point of the pin approximately ¼" (0.64cm) from the edge of the block.

2. Sew with a ¼" (0.64cm) seam. (Don't try following any of the printed lines of the paper template as a sewing guide.) Press the seam open. Repeat with two more blocks to make two half sun blocks.

3. Align the two halves, right sides together, and pin and sew with a ¼" (0.64cm) seam.

4. Press the seams open to reduce the bulk in the seams.

Alternate Blocks

Some of the quilts in this book use alternate blocks. These blocks are either half-square triangles (HST) or a half-square triangle with a "connector square," which is sometimes referred to as a "stitch and flip corner" or a "snowball corner." You are probably like us and not thrilled about working with ⅛" (0.05cm) cutting increments. So we cut the squares 1" (0.39cm) larger than the size of the finished half-square triangle (HST).

1. Cut two 7" (17.78cm) squares, or two 5" (12.7cm) squares, and align, right sides together. Draw a diagonal line from corner to corner using your favorite marking tool.

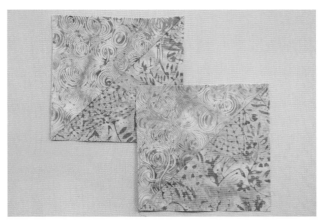

2. Sew ¼" (0.64cm) on both sides of the drawn line. Cut on the drawn line and press the seams to make two, half-square triangles. Trim the HST to 6½" (16.51cm), or 4½" (11.43cm).

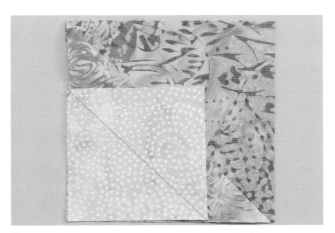

3. If you would like a little extra "kick," add a "connector square." The connector can be any size that you like. For the 6½" (16.51cm) blocks, we use either a 2½" (6.35cm) or 3½" (8.89cm) connector. Trim the HST block to the designated size before you add the connector square.

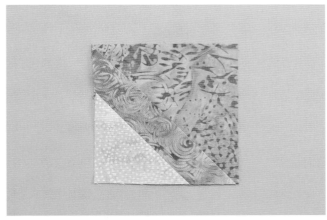

4. Place the connector square on the corner of the HST. Draw a diagonal line from corner to corner. Sew on the drawn line. Fold the square back on itself and press. Cut away the two layers underneath (connector fabric and HST fabric).

Make a Mini!

Many people refrain from foundation piecing because they feel that there is some fabric waste. The mini quilts use the scraps and cutaways from the 6" (15.24cm) blocks. In essence, you are cutting yourself a kit! Most of the cutaways can be used to piece the arcs. Your mini block will depend on how many cutaways you are able to use after making the bigger block. Use up what you can from your scraps and be creative if you need additional pieces to finish.

1. Refer to page 10 to make arc foundations for a mini New York Beauty Block. A template is provided on page 85 or use Frog Hollow Designs templates available at *www.froghollowdesigns.com.*

2. In this photo, the blue piece is a cutaway from the background spire of a trimmed 6" (15.24cm) block. The mini is made in the same manner as a 6" (15.24cm) block. Refer to pages 11–13, Piecing the Arc Foundations.

3. The purple piece is the cutaway from the spire.

4. Continue rolling, creasing, sewing and trimming the spire pieces all the way down the arc and press after each piece is sewn.

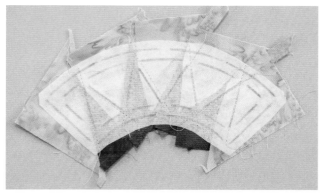

5. Turn the arc over and cut along the outer curved lines of the foundation. On the straight sides, leave an extra ¼" (0.64cm) to just under ½" (1.27cm). You will be able to adjust this allowance once you are familiar with the technique.

6. The arc foundation is trimmed before setting in the pie and the background pieces.

7. The final trim on the mini is done in the same way as a 6" (15.24cm) block, pages 18–19. But the diagonal line on the ruler will run between the two center spires.

8. Slide the ruler diagonally toward the bottom left corner of the block, watching the 4"(10.16cm) line on both sides of the ruler.

9. Stop when the ¾" (1.91cm) marks align on the seam lines of the arc and background. Trim the block on the top and right side of the ruler. Rotate the block 180° and trim remaining sides.

Finishing

You have worked hard on your blocks and you are probably anxious to get the top finished so you can work on the quilting!

Batting

We use and recommend Nature-Fil batting from Fairfield Processing for our projects. You are, of course, welcome to use your favorite batting product.

Quilting

To audition quilting designs, place a black and white image of the whole quilt or portions of the quilt in a cheap, clear page protector. Doodle some designs on the page protector, using a dry erase pen. You can wipe off the ink with a dry paper towel. Once you have a design that you like, make a photocopy of what you have done for reference.

Hanging Sleeve

The materials list for the quilt includes enough fabric to compensate for longarm quilting, binding cut at 2½" (6.35cm) by WOF, and enough extra to make a 4" (10.16cm) hanging sleeve.

Label

We design our labels in Word and then print them onto fabric. You can make your own or buy them commercially. Use a permanent marker to include the date the quilt was made. Whether it's for someone special or a special occasion, the label will be a remembrance of the maker...you!

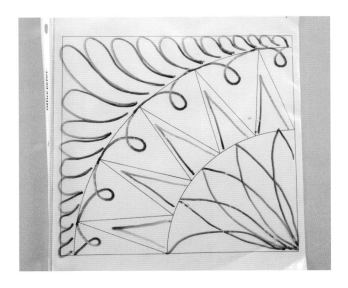

Adding Borders

Please take the time to measure your quilt before adding the borders. As longarm quilters, we have seen many beautiful quilts distorted when inaccurate borders are attached.

Sometimes the size of your quilt can change by the time you reach the final stage of adding borders. This change can occur because of all the seams involved in piecework. For this reason, it is a good idea to cut the borders to the size of your actual quilt, and not necessarily to the instructions of the pattern that you are using. We always cut our borders after we have pieced the quilt center.

We prefer to cut our borders along the straight of grain as opposed to the cross grain. The straight of grain is parallel to the selvage edge. We remove the selvage before cutting since this edge is a much tighter weave and is often made with a different color or thread weight.

Piecing Border/Sashing Strips

If you need to piece your border or sashing strips, We strongly suggest that you piece them using a diagonal seam as opposed to a straight seam. In this way, you are able to distribute the bulk of the seams underneath and get a straighter strip.

Adding a Solid Border/Sashing

Begin with a quilt top that is starched and pressed flat. Sliver trim the sides to get them straight. Measure the length and the width of the quilt top through the center to get the truest measurement.

Measure the quilt from top to bottom through the center of the quilt for the side borders. Fold the quilt top and the side borders in half, creasing the centers of each. Pin the border, right sides together, matching the creases. Sew a border to each side of the quilt. Starch the borders closed, then open and press again.

Once the side borders are attached, repeat to add the top and bottom border. Measure the width, including the side borders, through the center of the quilt. Pin the borders to the top and bottom of the quilt center, right sides together, and sew. Starch the borders closed, then open and press again.

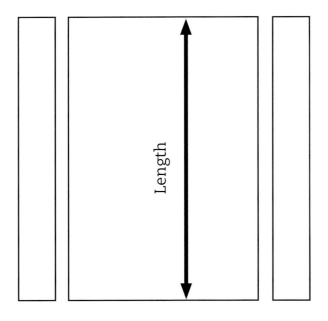

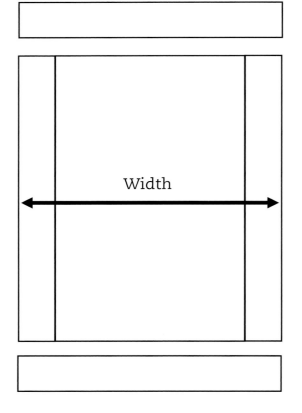

Jazz It Up!

Couching

Couching is a fun and easy way to accent pieced lines or create movement in a quilt. The term "couching" refers to the process of stitching, usually with a zig-zag stitch, over a thicker thread or yarn.

Choosing Your Fiber

You can couch over all types of threads and yarns, even rickrack or ribbon. In these projects, we used eyelash yarn (so called because of the little threads sticking out in all directions) and some nubby yarns. You might want to hold several up to your quilt to see which type might complement the design. It will require about 36" (91.44cm) to sew completely around the outer "ring" of the New York Beauty blocks (the outside of the spires) or about 22" (55.88cm) to sew around the inner "ring" (the joined pies).

When to Couch

You might wonder whether you should couch first or quilt first. The answer is that either might work. For these quilts, we waited until the blocks were pieced together and the quilting was completed. It can be difficult to work around the couching yarns, especially if you are using an edge-to-edge quilting design or have used many loose eyelash yarns which can get caught in the foot or in the quilting stitches. If you wish to complete the couching before you quilt, you might need to use a machine-embroidery stabilizer behind the block to avoid puckering.

Presser Feet

Various presser feet are available for sewing machines. Most often used are either an open-toe foot or a foot designed with a hole in it for couching. You might want to try out the yarn and the foot to see which works best. The open toe foot, on the right, works well on specialty yarns, and it is easy to see where the yarn and stitches are located. It doesn't get caught on the fibers, especially if you are working with a bumpy yarn or one with long eyelash strands. The couching foot, on the left, works well with straight, smooth yarns or threads, such as perle cotton or thicker ribbon yarns.

Thread

Choose a top thread to match your yarn or fiber. If you prefer, this is a good time to break out the shiny rayon or metallic threads if you prefer a contrast or want to add more sparkle. Invisible thread could also be used if you don't want the stitches to show at all. Bobbin thread can match the top thread. If you are sewing on a finished quilt, you could also match the bobbin thread to the quilt backing.

Stitch Width and Length

We suggest making a small quilt sandwich with a piece of fabric and batting to test the stitch width and length.

Start with the default zig-zag settings on your machine. Zig-zag for a few inches on a length of the yarn to be used. Usually, the width should be adjusted so that the needle just clears the yarn on both sides. You could increase the width if you want the top thread to show more. Stitch length should not be so short that the yarn is completely covered, and may be a little longer than normal if you are using a fluffy or eyelash yarn so that the fibers are not compressed. Adjust the stitch length until you are pleased with the effect, then write down the setting you like.

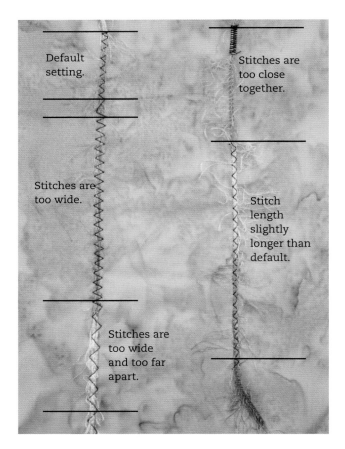

Default setting.

Stitches are too close together.

Stitches are too wide.

Stitch length slightly longer than default.

Stitches are too wide and too far apart.

How to Add Couching to Your Quilt Top

1. To add couching to the outer "ring" of New York Beauty blocks, begin at the middle of an arc. The join will be less visible there. Leave several inches of yarn loose and begin sewing.

2. Sew slowly, adjusting the yarn every few stitches to follow the curve of the arc. Continue stitching all the way around the circle. When you reach the beginning, continue to stitch for about ½" (1.27 cm), overlapping the previous stitching. Use a locking stitch or reverse stitch for a couple of stitches.

3. Trim the yarn close to the stitching.

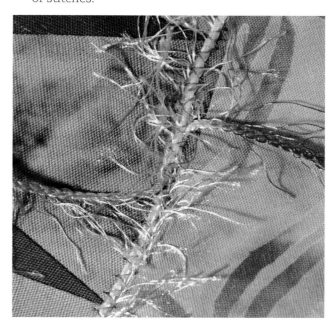

Add Some Bling Using Sparkly Tulle

Tulle is a fine netting, often used in bridal veils, which comes in a rainbow of colors. It can be purchased by the yard or in 6" rolls. The butterfly wings on "Strawberry Fields," page 46, feature a technique that uses tulle to hold down sparkly fibers.

As far as color goes, we most often use black for the projects, since the black makes the colors of the fibers beneath it stand out. White tends to blend all of the colors together, which could work if you are going for a pastel theme. As an alternative, you could use tulle in a color to match the color of the pie shapes.

Angelina Fibers and Metallic Thread

Our favorite item for extra sparkle is called "Angelina fibers," which are very fine fibers cut from a metallic polyester sheet. You can also use bits of shiny fabric or random lengths of glittery or metallic thread. It's a great time to use up those threads that your machine doesn't "like."

We like to embellish the blocks before they are sewn together, making it easier to couch or sew around the tulle.

Embellishing the Butterfly Wings

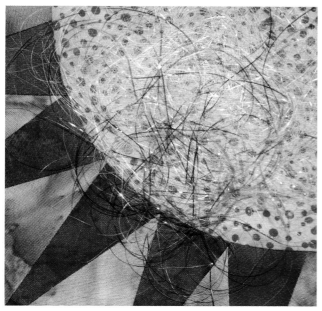

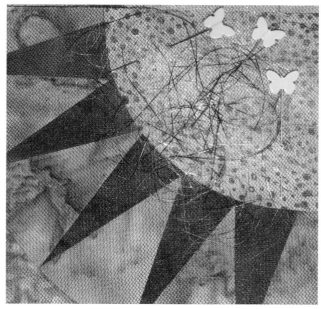

1. Spring your bling on the butterfly wing (pie shape)! Spread Angelina fiber evenly over the pie, and let sections of the fabric peek through. When you think there is enough, cover the pie shape with a piece of tulle at least 1" (2.54cm) larger all around.

2. Loosely pin the tulle in place. Straight stitch ⅛" (0.32cm) from the straight edges of the pie shape, then along the curve between the bottom of the spires and the pie shape.

3. Trim the tulle even with the straight edges of the pie shape and as close to the curve as you can without cutting the stitches. Then, zigzag stitch over the curved edge to secure the tulle in place.

4. If you have chosen to embellish the blocks after the entire quilt is quilted, follow steps 1–3, and add additional stitching or scatter beads across the tulle to keep it in place.

Adding Silk Flowers

"Silk" flowers from a craft store can be a simple but lively addition to your quilt. We added a silk flower garden to "Strawberry Fields," but you could also add flowers to the pies of any New York Beauty block. Flowers should be added after the quilting and binding are completed. This technique is best suited to quilts that will not be washed.

Preparing the Flowers

Choose flowers in an appropriate size and color range to complement your quilt design. Consider where you want to place the flowers. Choose the first flower and remove it from its plastic stem. The flower will pull off easily. Remove the plastic center section holding the petal layers together.

Attaching the Flowers

Option 1—Sewing

Place the flower on the quilt and pin lightly as needed. Use a few hand or machine stitches to secure the center of the flower. Cover the hole left from the removal of the plastic center with a few beads or a button.

Option 2—Gluing

Since this quilt will not be washable, use of hot glue or any appropriate fabric glue is a second option. Be careful to keep the glue away from the center. It will be difficult to bead or sew a button through the hard glue.

Embellishing with Leaves

Most bunches of silk flowers also include leaves, which can be included in the design. The leaves can be glued or sewn in place. We like to sew them down with a few lines of stitching along the "vein" lines, leaving the edges loose for more 3D texture.

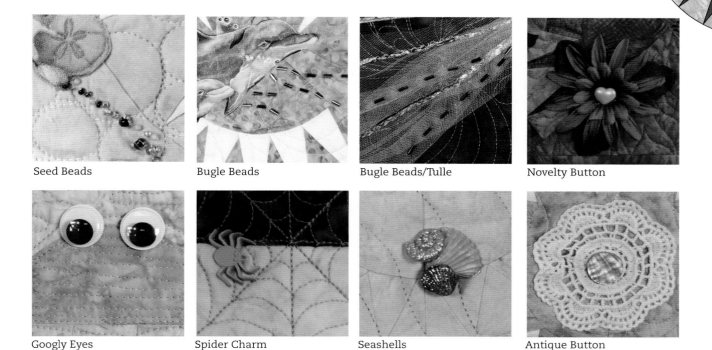

Seed Beads

Bugle Beads

Bugle Beads/Tulle

Novelty Button

Googly Eyes

Spider Charm

Seashells

Antique Button

Beads, Buttons and Charms

Beads, buttons and charms can add texture and depth to the completed quilt. It's difficult to quilt around these items, so it's best to add them after quilting and binding are finished.

Choosing Beads

- Any type of bead can be used to add color and movement to your quilt. Seed beads of various sizes and colors were combined to create the "sand" on Crown Point Crawlers, page 38.

- Bugle beads were used to enhance the "waves" of Crown Point Crawlers.

- Seed beads and bugle beads were used in Scarsdale Stars, page 72, to anchor the tulle swathes and to add to the galaxy effect.

Buttons and Novelty Items

Other items can be used to add movement and enhance the theme of the quilt: charms, novelty items, googly eyes, spiders, seashells, and antique buttons.

Applying Beads the Simple Way

Thread: Either beading thread (Nymo is a commonly available brand) or two strands of 50 weight thread matching the background color can be used. Since these quilts were made to hang on the wall, we used cotton thread to match the background or the beads. If your project will be quilted and laundered often, or you have made a wearable piece, you might prefer to use beading thread which will wear better under stress.

Needles: We use John James size 10 straw needles for all hand sewing (beading, binding, appliqué). Any hand sewing needle or beading needle that will fit through the bead and accommodate the size of the thread will do.

Stitching: A simple stab stitch was used for beading these quilts. Many other stitches can also be used.

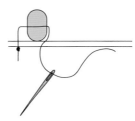

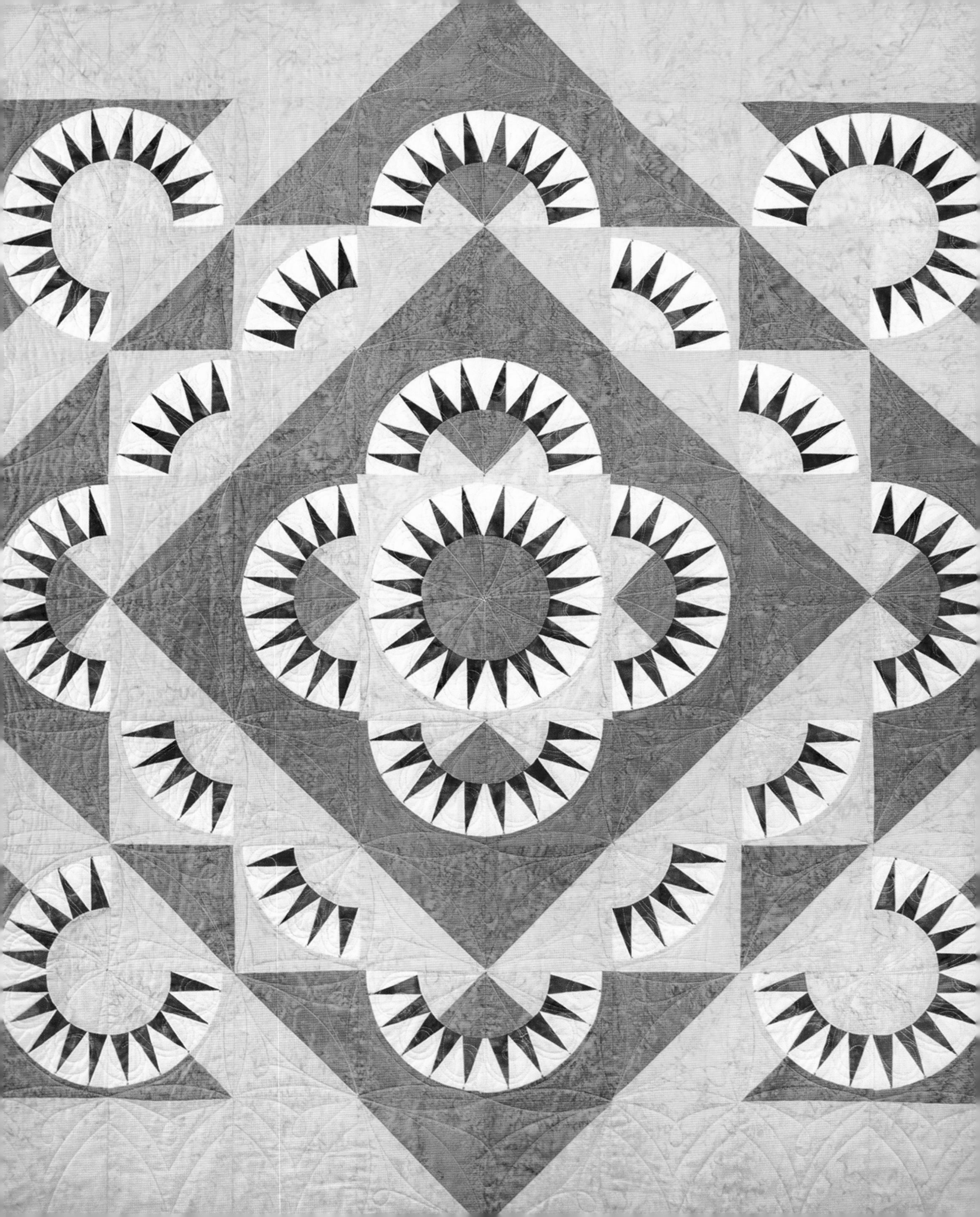

Projects

Crown Point Crawlers

Being so close to the coast, seafood can be found in lots of restaurants in Crown Point. Some make it a tradition to fill up on crab before heading back home.

Arc Foundation Requirements

(48) New York Beauty arc foundations

Fabric Requirements

- ¼ yard (22.86cm) coral for the crab
- 1½ yards (137.16cm) white for the waves
- 2 yards (182.88cm) beige for the sand
- 1 yard (68.58cm) dark blue for the ocean
- 1 yard (68.58cm) dark teal for the ocean and binding
- 1 yard (91.44cm) blue-green for the ocean
- 1½ yards (137.16cm) turquoise for the ocean
- 1¾ yards (160.02cm) for backing and hanging sleeve fabric

WOF = Width of fabric

Cutting

From the coral fabric, cut:
(2) 4½" (11.43cm) squares
(8) 2½" x 3½" (6.35 x 8.89cm) rectangles

From the white fabric, cut:
(220) 2½" x 3½" (6.35 x 8.89cm) rectangles

From the beige fabric, cut;
(15) 8" (20.32cm) squares. From the squares, cut;
    (15) background shapes. From leftover fabric, cut:
    (11) 4½" (11.43cm) squares
(10) 2½" x 3½" (6.35 x 8.89cm) rectangles for spires
(90) 3" x 4" (7.62 x 10.16cm) rectangles for background spires

From the dark blue fabric, cut:
(3) 8" (20.32cm) squares From each square, cut:
    (1) background shape for a total of 3
    (1) 4½" (11.43cm) square for a total of 3 pies
(3) 4½" (11.43cm) squares for pies
(36) 3" x 4" (7.62 x 10.16cm) rectangles for background spires

From the dark teal fabric, cut:
(3) 8" (20.32cm) squares. From each square, cut:
    (1) background shape for a total of 3
    (1) 4½" (11.43cm) square for a total of 3 pies
(1) 4½" (11.43cm) square for pies
(24) 3" x 4" (7.62 x 10.16cm) rectangles for spires
(5) 2½" (6.35cm) x WOF strips for binding

From the blue-green fabric, cut:
(10) 8" (20.32cm) squares. From each of 9 squares, cut:
    (1) background shape for a total of 9
    (1) 4½" (11.43cm) square for a total of 9 pies

    From remaining square, cut:
    (2) 4½" (11.43cm) squares for pies
(66) 3" x 4" (7.62 x 10.16cm) rectangles for spires

From the turquoise fabric, cut:
(18) 8" (20.32cm) squares. From each square, cut:
    (18) background shapes. From leftover fabric, cut:
    (14) 4½" (11.43cm) squares for pies
(72) 3" x 4" (7.62 x 10.16cm) rectangles for spires
(2) 2½" x 3½" (6.35 x 6.35cm) rectangles for spires

Construction

Following the instructions on page 10–19, make the following New York Beauty block combinations.

Make 3
dark blue for
the pie,
background and
background
spires

Make 3
dark blue for
the pie, and
background spires,
and dark teal for
background

Make 4
dark teal for
the pie and
background spires,
and the blue-green
for the background

36" x 48" (91.44 x 121.92cm)
Made by Linda J. Hahn, Palm Bay, FL
Quilted by Jodi Robinson, Enon Valley, PA
Embellishments by Deborah G. Stanley, Matawan, NJ

Make 5
blue-green for the
pie, background and
background spires

Make 6
blue-green for the
pies, background
spires, and turquoise
for background

Make 11
turquoise for the
pie, background
and background
spires

Make 3
turquoise for the pie
and beige for the
background spires,
and background.

Make 9
beige for the pie,
background spires,
and background

Make 1
beige for the
background,
pie, background
spires and four of
the spires. Use the
coral for one spire.

Make 1
beige for the
background,
pie, background
spires and four of
the spires. Use the
coral for one spire.

Make 1
beige for the
background,
background spires
and two of the spires.
Use the coral for three
spires and the pie.

Make 1
light blue for
the background,
background spires
and two of the
spires. Use the
coral for three
spires and the pie.

Quilt Assembly

1. Following the Quilt Assembly Diagram, lay out the blocks as shown. Sew the blocks into rows and sew the rows together to finish the quilt top.

2. Layer the back, batting, and quilt top. Quilt as desired and add the binding.

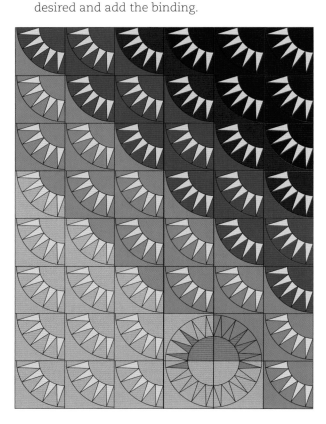

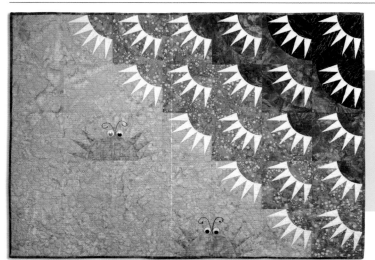

Feelin' Crabby

Linda added a second crab into this design and used solid 6½" (16.51cm) squares of "sand" instead of New York Beauty blocks.

42" x 30" (106.68 x 76.20cm)

Made by Linda Hahn

Quilted by Jodi Robinson, Enon Valley, PA

Plattsburgh Pinchers Mini

Our friend Roxanne Kermidas took the cutaways and scraps from the main quilt and created this cute mini! Her crab features shell buttons and wiggle eyes.

24" X 32" (60.96 x 81.28cm)

Made by Roxanne Kermidas, Palm Bay, FL

Quilted by Jodi Robinson, Enon Valley, PA

Embellishments by Roxanne Kermidas,
    Palm Bay, FL

Jazz It Up!

What we did:
We found some seashell, fish, dolphin and sea turtle novelty fabrics that we fussy cut, fused and sewed to the quilt. We added beads and charms to enhance the "sand" and "waves," giving them a sparkley effect.

Other ideas:
Add some real seashells or some larger sea creature charms. You could also sew down some novelty yarns in swirls for a "seaweed" effect.

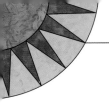

Peekskill Peepers

Peekskill, New York, is situated along the Hudson River.
Bays and ponds dot the area and one doesn't have to walk
far to hear the sounds of frogs hidden in the grass around the water.

Arc Foundation Requirements
(39) New York Beauty arc foundations

Fabric Requirements
- 3¼ yards (297.18cm) blue fabric for background
- 2¾ yards (251.46cm) assorted greens for spires, pies, frogs, and weeds
- 2¼ yards (205.74cm) light green for background spire
- 1 yard (91.44cm) assorted pinks/purples fabric for waterlilies
- ¼ yard (22.86cm) gold fabric for waterlily centers
- 2 yards (182.88cm) fusible 18"-wide (45.72cm) web (Steam-A-Seam®)
- ½ yard (45.72cm) fabric for binding
- (2) 1½ yard cuts (137.16cm) for backing

WOF = Width of fabric

Cutting
From the blue fabric, cut:
(39) 8" (20.32cm) squares

(31) 6½" (16.51cm) squares

From the assorted green fabrics, cut:
(195) 2½" x 3½" (6.35 x 8.89cm) spire rectangles

(39) 4½" (11.43cm) squares for pies

* Use leftover pieces for frogs and weeds

From light green fabric, cut:
(234) 3" x 4" (7.62 x 10.16cm) rectangles for background spires

From the pink and purple fabric, cut:
Each waterlily flower uses a 6½" (16.51cm) square and a 3" (7.62cm) square.
You can choose to add as many or as few as you like. (See templates, pages 88–89.)

From the gold fabric, cut:
3" (7.62cm) squares for each of your waterlilies

From the binding fabric, cut:
(6) 2½" (6.35cm) x WOF strips

Construction
Following the instructions on pages 10–19, make a total of (39) New York Beauty blocks

Make 39 with assorted greens

Assembly
1. Arrange the New York Beauty blocks and the 6½" (16.51cm) squares of blue on your design wall. Use our layout or feel free to make your own arrangement.

2. Assemble into the quilt top and set aside while you prepare the waterlily flowers, weeds and frogs.

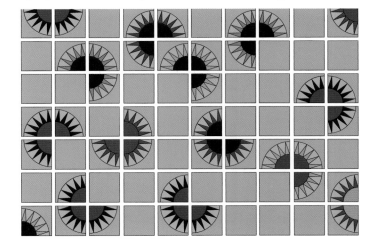

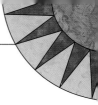

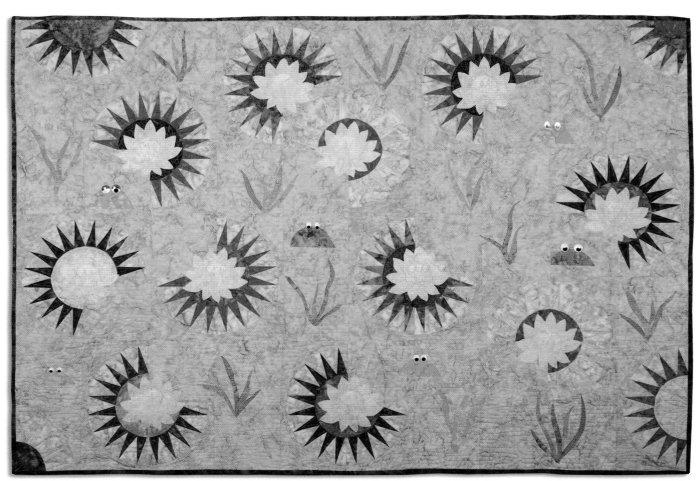

60" x 42" (152.40 x 106.68cm)
Made and quilted by Linda J. Hahn, Palm Bay, FL

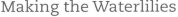

Making the Weeds

Fuse a variety of rectangles of greens. Freehand cut as many weeds as you would like. Make sure that you vary the lengths and widths of the stems. I randomly cut and placed them down until each cluster was pleasing to my eye. Fuse the pieces down according to manufacturer's instructions.

Making the Waterlilies

1. Trace and fuse the waterlily flower pieces, (see templates, pages 88–89) onto the pink and purple fabrics. Cut out and set aside. Then trace, fuse and cut out the gold flower centers.

2. Assemble the flowers by placing the gold center onto the larger flower piece and covering it with the smaller flower piece. Lay them out on your quilt top in the centers of the New York Beauty block clusters. When you are happy with the arrangement, follow the manufacturer's instructions and fuse the pieces to the quilt top.

Making the Frogs

Fuse a few squares of green in a variety of sizes. Freehand cut half moon shapes. Be sure to make some large, some small, and some short, for a nice variety. Fuse into place on the quilt top. Add the wiggle eyes Make left eye above, black after the quilting is done. Vary the eye sizes and placement (some close together, some high on the face, some lower). Attach the eyes with a craft glue.

Appliqué

1. All the fused pieces were raw edge appliquéd and quilted down close to the edge, and then we did some quilting in the pieces, as well. The weeds were also raw edge appliquéd/quilted down.

2. Layer, baste, and quilt as desired and bind. After the quilt is completed, add the wiggly eyes with a craft glue. Vary size and placement. Don't forget your label.

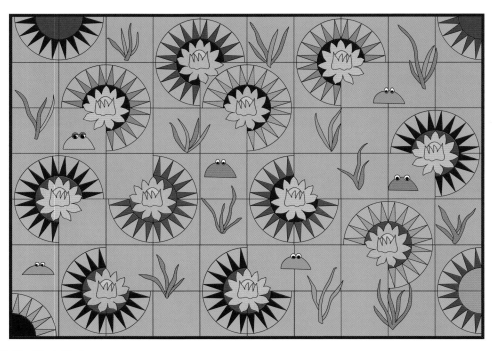

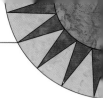

Tarrytown Tadpoles Mini

32" x 16 " (81.28 x 40.64cm)

Made and quilted by Linda J. Hahn, Palm Bay, FL

Strawberry Fields

Strawberry Fields is known as a meditative area in Central Park. The quiet spot features beautiful blooms and butterflies all along the path in the warmer months.

Arc Foundation Requirements
(10) Three Spire New York Beauty arcs (Split spire)

(11) Five Spire New York Beauty Arcs

Fabric Requirements
- 3¼ yards (297.18cm) blue for background spires and background
- 1¼ yards (114.30cm) assorted greens for background spires, background, and triangles
- From scraps or your stash, use assorted colors to cut spire and pie pieces listed below in Cutting.
- (2) 1½ yard (137.16cm) cuts for backing and hanging sleeve
- ½ yard (45.72cm) for binding

WOF = Width of fabric

Cutting
From the blue fabric, cut:

(29) 6½" (16.51cm) squares for background

(8) 7" (17.78cm) squares cut in half on the diagonal

(15) 8" (20.32cm) squares. From the squares, cut: (15) background shapes

(40) 3½" x 4" (8.89 x 10.16cm) rectangles for butterfly background spires

(30) 3" x 4" (7.62 x 10.16cm) rectangles for flower background spires

From assorted colors, cut the following, matching colors within each set, and keeping sets organized by color.

(3) Sets of (3) 4½" squares (11.43cm) for flower pies

(3) Sets of (15) 2½" x 3½" (6.35 x 8.89cm) rectangles for flower spires

(2) 4½" squares (11.43cm) for single arc flower pies

(2) Sets of (5) 2½" x 3½" (6.35 x 8.89cm) rectangles for single flower spires

(5) Sets of (2) 4½" squares (11.43cm) for butterfly pies

(5) Sets of (6) 2½" x 4" (6.35 x 10.16cm) rectangles for split spire butterfly wings using DARKER colors

(5) Sets of (6) 2½" x 4" (6.35 x 10.16cm) rectangles for split spire butterfly wings using LIGHTER colors

(5) 2" x 5" rectangles (5.08 x 12.70cm) for butterfly bodies

From the assorted green fabrics, cut:

(6) 8" (20.32cm) squares. From the squares, cut: (6) background shapes

(5) 7" (17.78cm) squares cut in half on the diagonal

(36) 3" x 4" (7.62 x 10.16cm) rectangles for background spires

From the binding fabric, cut:

(5) 2½" (6.35cm) x WOF strips

Construction
1. Following the instructions on page 11, Piecing the Arc Foundations, make the following New York Beauty five spire arcs. Refer to the illustrations below for color combinations.

2. Using two sets of (3) matching pies and flower spires, make 2 sets of (2) New York Beauty arcs, using a variety of greens for the background and background spires.

3. From the third set of matching pies and flower spires, make 1 each of the pie/spire combinations, but use blue background spires and blue backgrounds.

Make 2 of each

Make 1 of each

51" x 43" (129.54 x 109.22cm)
Made and quilted by Linda J. Hahn, Palm Bay, FL
Embellishments by Deborah G. Stanley, Matawan, NJ

4. Make two single New York Beauty flower arcs, using scraps for spires and pies, and the blue as background and background spires.

5. Using the dark and light sets of 2½" x 4" (6.85 x 10.16cm) rectangles for split spire butterfly wings, sew a dark and light rectangle together on one long side. Press the seams open. Repeat with all rectangles to make (30) dark/light spires.

6. To make the butterfly wings, use the dark/light spires from step 5, the 3½" x 4" (8.89 x 10.16cm) blue background rectangles, and (10) blue background shapes, to make 1 set of 5 colorways. (Three spire arcs are made in the same way as the five spire arcs.) These blocks are embellished after the quilt top is constructed.

7. Referring to the quilt assembly, lay out the New York Beauty flower blocks, butterfly wing spire blocks, and the 6½" (16.51cm) background blocks. Add a triangle cut from the 7" (17.78cm) squares to the ends of each row. The top two blue corners will be a bit large, and you will need to trim them once the quilt is assembled.

8. Butterfly Bodies: Following the manufacturer's instructions, apply fusible web to the back of the (5) 2" x 5" (5.08 x 12.70cm) rectangles.

9. From the step 8 rectangles, freehand cut a long oval to use as the butterfly body. Fuse to the quilt top between the butterfly wings and straight sew or zig-zag stitch to secure.

10. Layer, quilt, and bind the quilt before adding any embellishments.

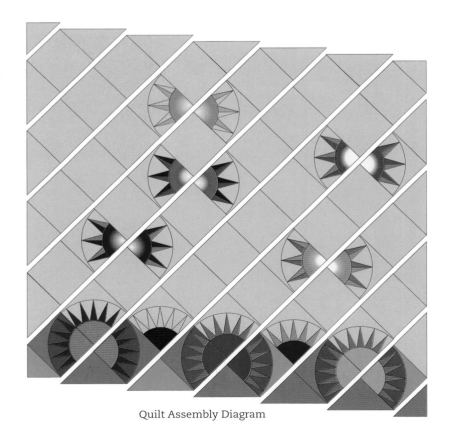

Quilt Assembly Diagram

Strawberry Mini

36" x 36" (91.44 x 91.44cm)

Made and quilted by Linda J. Hahn, Palm Bay, FL

Embellishments by
   Roxanne Kermidas, Palm Bay, FL

Jazz It Up!

What we did:
Hand embroidered antennae for each butterfly

Added:
- Sparkle to the wings with Angelina fibers
- Beads to the wings
- Silk flowers
- Buttons and beads for the flower centers

Roxbury Rainbow

When visiting Roxbury, a requirement is to slow down and take in the scenery, from rolling hills to the Catskill mountains. In the fall, the area is awash with color...yellow, gold, and red leaves contrast with expansive blue skies.

Arc Foundation Requirements

(36) New York Beauty arc foundations

Fabric Requirements

- 1½ yards (137.16cm) black fabric for spires
- 2 yards (182.88cm) white fabric for background spires
- ¼ yard (22.86cm) each of (9) assorted solid colors
- ⅓ yard (30.45cm) each of (9) assorted white on black fabrics for background
- ⅓ yard (30.45cm) each of (9) assorted black on white fabrics for background
- ½ yard (45.72cm) for binding
- 1⅓ yards (121.89cm) fabric for backing and hanging sleeve

WOF = Width of fabric

Cutting

From the black fabric, cut:
(180) 2½" x 3½" (6.35 x 8.89cm) spire rectangles

From the white fabric, cut:
(216) 3" x 4" (7.62 x 10.16cm) spire rectangles

From each of the (9) assorted solid color fabrics, cut:
(1) Set of (4) 4½" (11.43cm) squares for pies

From each of the (9) assorted white on black fabrics, cut:
(1) 8" (20.32cm) square
(1) 9½" (24.13cm) square

From each of the (9) assorted black on white fabrics, cut:
(1) 8" (20.32cm) square
(1) 9½" (24.13cm) square

From the binding fabric, cut:
(5) 2½" (6.35cm) x WOF strips

Construction

1. Begin by pinning together (4) 4½" (11.43cm) squares of matching colors, for a total of 9 sets.

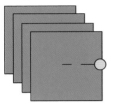

Make 9

2. Pin together the matching 9½" (24.13cm) square and 8" (20.32cm) square of white on black fabrics. You will have (9) sets.

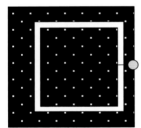

Make 9

3. Pin together the matching 9½" (24.13cm) square and 8" (20.32cm) square of black on white fabrics. You will have (9) sets.

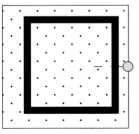

Make 9

4. For each of the 4½" (11.43cm) color sets, follow instructions, pages 10–19, to make (36) pie/arc units. Set aside.

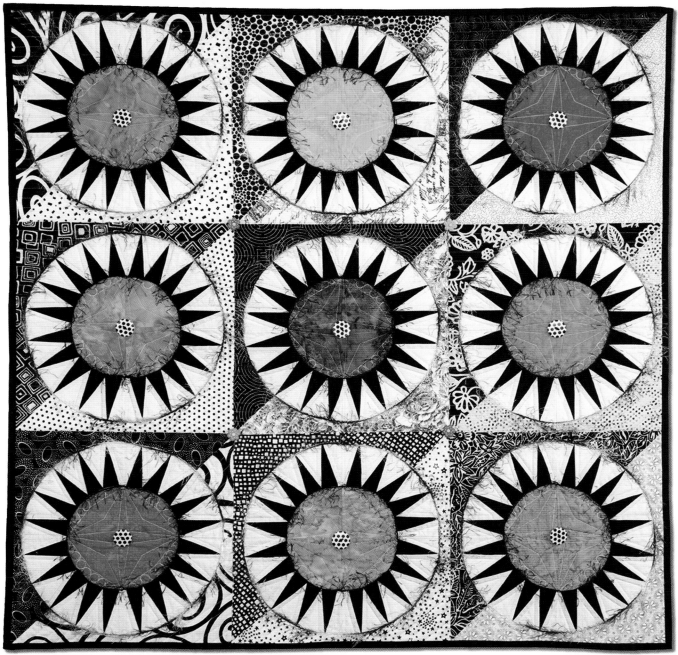

36" x 36" (91.44 x 91.44cm)
Made by Nancy Rock, Edison, NJ
Quilted by Jodi Robinson, Enon Valley, PA

Make the Half Square Triangles (HST)

1. Working with the matched pairs, choose one set from each of the black on white and white on black squares. Set the other block pairs aside.

2. Using the 9½" (24.13cm) square from each set, pin the squares right sides together. Draw a line from corner to corner and sew ¼" (0.64cm) on both sides of the line. Cut on the drawn line and press the seam open. Using starch for this step is helpful.

3. Cut two background pieces from the half-square triangles from step 2, using the template, page 87. Be careful when placing the template down on the half-square triangles. Make sure the fabric is going in the correct direction.

4. From the 8" (20.32cm) squares of the sets, cut out a background from each, using the template on page 87. Repeat steps 2-4, with the rest of the 8" (20.32cm) and 9½" (24.13cm) squares.

5. Following the instructions, Adding a Split Background, on page 20, sew the background pieces to the pie/arc pieces. Make a total of 9 blocks.

6. Sew the blocks together in rows. Sew the rows together to complete the quilt top.

7. Layer, baste, quilt and bind the quilt.

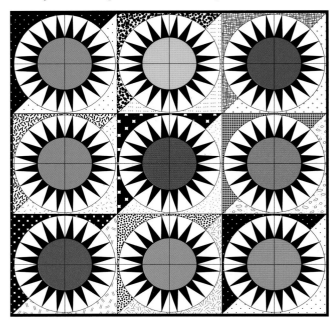

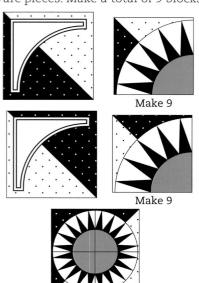

Make 9

Make 9

Alternate Setting Ideas

1. Purchase an extra 1½ yards (3.81cm) of black fabric and cut sashing strips to quarter the New York Beauty blocks. Cut strips 2" x 6½" (5.08 x 16.51cm). Cut 2" (5.08cm) cornerstones, using a ¼ yard (22.86cm) of contrasting color. Bind the quilt or add a black border.

2. To create an illusion of the blocks being skewed and also create a secondary pattern, cut the HST's with the black or white on the same side of the template, for example, black always on the left side. You will need to make (36) 9" (22.86cm) HST's from black and white fabric combinations.

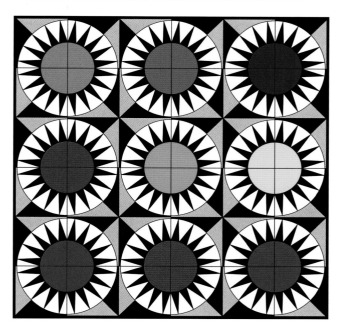

Jazz It Up!

What we did:

We couched black eyelash yarn around the inner edge of spire circles and variegated yarn around the outer edge of spire circles. Black and white buttons and small flower buttons were added to the block centers and intersections for interest.

Other ideas:

Practice free-motion skills by quilting each set of blocks with a different design. Add beads, buttons or charms to accent the blocks. Add additional couched yarns as desired.

Nassau Neutral

With the Atlantic Ocean on one side and the Long Island Sound on the other, Nassau is a quick twenty-minute drive from New York City. Nassau Neutral replicates the colors of the many architectural treasures that fill this small but impressive historical town.

Arc Foundation Requirements
(16) New York Beauty Arc Foundations

Fabric Requirements
- ⅝ yard (57.15cm) solid black Fabric 1 for spires
- 1 yard (91.44cm) solid cream Fabric 2 for background spires
- ⅜ yard (34.29cm) Fabric 3 for pies.
  You can choose a fabric that blends with the background strips.

For the background strip set, choose a gradation of a color family for fabrics 4-8. For our project, we chose tan to brown. Piece the strips if necessary.

- ⅝ yard (57.15cm) Fabric 4 for strip 1
- ½ yard (45.72cm) Fabric 5 for strip 2
- ½ yard (45.72cm) Fabric 6 for strip 3
- ½ yard (45.72cm) Fabric 7 for strip 4
- ⅝ yard (57.15cm) Fabric 8 for strip 5
- ½ yard (45.72cm) for binding
- 2 yards (182.88cm) for backing and hanging sleeve fabric

WOF = Width of fabric

Cutting
From Fabric 1, cut:
(80) 2½" x 3½" (6.35 x 8.89cm) rectangles for spires

From Fabric 2, cut:
(96) 3" x 4" (7.62 x 10.16cm) background spires

From Fabric 3, cut:
(16) 4½" (11.43cm) squares for pies

From Fabric 4, cut:
(2) 8" (20.32cm) squares
(1) 2½" x 6½" (6.35 x 16.51cm) strip for background
(1) 6½" x 44½" (16.51 x 113.03cm) strip

From Fabric 5, cut:
(4) 8" (20.32cm) squares for background
(1) 6½" x 30½" (16.51 x 77.47cm) strip
(2) 2½" x 6½" (6.35 x 16.51cm) strips

From Fabric 6, cut:
(4) 8" (20.32cm) squares for background
(1) 2½" x 6½" (6.35 x 16.51cm) strip
(2) 6½" x 16½" (16.51 x 41.91cm) strips

From Fabric 7, cut:
(4) 8" (20.32cm) squares for background
(2) 2½" x 6½" (6.35 x 16.51cm) strips
(1) 6½" x 30½" (16.51 x 77.47cm) strip

From Fabric 8, cut:
(2) 8" (20.32cm) squares for background
(1) 2½" x 6½" (6.35 x 16.51cm) strips
(1) 6½" x 44½" (16.51 x 113.03cm) strip

From the binding fabric, cut:
(5) 2½" (6.35cm) x WOF strips

Construction
1. Following the instructions for making the basic New York Beauty block on pages 10–19, make the following:

Make 2
using Fabric 4 as
the background

30" x 60" (76.20 x 152.40cm)
Made by Janet Byard, Lawrenceville, NJ
Quilted by Jodi Robinson, Enon Valley, PA
Embellishments by Deborah Stanley, Matawan, NJ

Make 4
using Fabric 5 as
the background

Make 4
using Fabric 6 as
the background

Make 4
using Fabric 7 as
the background

Make 2
using Fabric 8 as
the background

2. Lay out the blocks and the cut fabric strips on your design wall, referring to the Quilt Assembly Diagram for placement. Sew the blocks into the strips and then sew the strips together to complete the quilt top. Layer, baste, and quilt as desired.

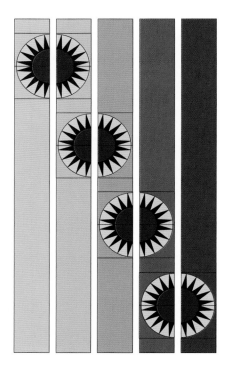

Quilt Assembly Diagram

Jazz It Up!

What we did:

We couched eyelash yarn around outer edge of the spire circles, and variegated yarn around inner edge of spire circles. Beads were added, following the quilting lines within the center area of pies. Variegated yarn was couched to accent the vertical dividing lines.

Other ideas:

Practice your free-motion quilting skills by using five different quilting designs, one for each fabric strip. Use buttons, charms, larger beads or fusible appliqué in each block circle.

Spiders of Sleepy Hollow

In Sleepy Hollow, New York, Halloween is the perfect setting for these 10-legged monsters! It's believed that Ichabod Crane, the lead character from "The Legend of Sleepy Hollow," was deathly afraid of spiders. But these little New York Beauty critters are nothing but friendly.

Arc Foundation Requirements
(12) New York Beauty arc foundations

Fabric Requirements
- 1¼ yards (114.30cm) black for nine-patch blocks and spiders
- 3⅝ yards (331.47cm) cream for nine-patch blocks, background spires, and squares
- ¼ yard (22.86cm) olive green for nine-patch blocks
- ½ yard (45.72cm) orange for nine-patch block
- ¾ yard (68.58cm) purple for nine-patch blocks and inner border
- 1 yard (91.44cm) black print for outer border
- ½ yard (45.72cm) for binding
- (2) cuts of 2 yards (182.88cm) each for backing and hanging sleeve

WOF = Width of fabric

Cutting
From the black fabric, cut:
(5) 2½" (6.35cm) x WOF strips
(60) 2½" x 3½" (6.35 x 8.89cm) rectangles for spires
(12) 4½" (11.43cm) squares for pies

From the cream fabric, cut:
(12) 7½" (19.05cm) squares cut once, diagonally
(13) 6½" (16.51cm) squares
(12) 8" (20.32cm) squares
(72) 3" x 4" (7.62 x 10.16cm) rectangles for background
(11) 2½" (6.35cm) x WOF strips

From the olive green fabric, cut:
(2) 2½" (6.35cm) x WOF strips

From the orange fabric, cut:
(5) 2½" (6.35cm) x WOF strips

From the purple fabric, cut:
(7) 2½" (6.35cm) x WOF strips

From the black print fabric, cut:
(6) 5" (12.70cm) x WOF strips

From the binding fabric, cut:
(5) 2½" (6.35cm) x WOF strips

Construction
1. Follow the instructions on pages 10–19, to make (12) New York Beauty blocks.

Make 12

2. Using the 2½" (6.35cm) x WOF strips, make the following strip sets, and then cross-cut the strip sets into 2½" (6.35cm) segments.

Make 5   72

strip sets of black, cream and orange

Make 1½   18

strip sets of cream, green and cream

62" x 62" (157.48 x 157.48cm)
Made by Linda J. Hahn, Palm Bay, FL
Quilted by Jodi Robinson, Enon Valley, PA

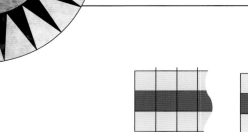

Make 1½   18

strips sets of cream,
purple and cream

3. Make (18) blocks of each coloring, paying attention to the position of the black and orange fabrics in each block.

Make 18 of each

Assembly

1. This quilt is assembled on point using the half-square triangles cut from the 7½" (19.05cm) squares for the setting and corner triangles. These half-square triangles are cut a little larger so that you have some "wiggle" room when you trim.

2. Lay out the quilt following the Quilt Assembly Diagram and sew together in diagonal rows, adding the cream 6½" (16.51cm) squares on each corner, and the setting triangles where indicated.

3. Trim away the excess setting and corner triangle fabric, leaving a ¼" (0.64cm) seam allowance so you can add the borders.

4. It is important to measure your quilt and cut the borders according to your measurements. Refer to Adding Borders, page 27, for instructions on measuring and adding borders.

5. Piece together the border strips and sew the 2½" (6.35cm) purple side borders, followed by the top and bottom purple borders. Press the top and re-measure (being careful not to stretch) to get the measurement for the 5" black border strips. Piece the black strips together. Cut to size and sew to the sides, followed by the top and bottom borders.

6. Layer, baste and quilt as desired. Add the binding.

Quilt Assembly Diagram

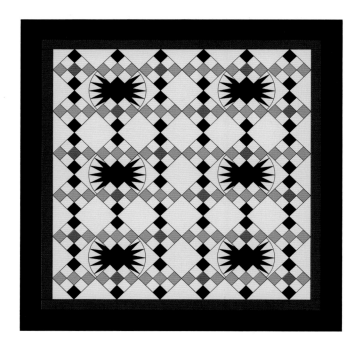

Jazz It Up!

What we did:

We found some interesting scary eyes for the spiders at our local craft store. We also found some small plastic spiders to attach in the spider web quilting by Jodi Robinson.

Other ideas:

Add some hand embroidered or beaded spiders and/or webs, 3D spider legs using pipe cleaners, or any small Halloween decorations that you may find at craft stores.

Ballston Spa Blues

The blues in this New York Beauty quilt could be the colors we think of when we think of water. The village of Ballston Spa was known for its healing mineral springs that still flow today for visitors who wish to drink from these cold, clear springs.

Arc Foundation Requirements
(16) New York Beauty blocks
(48) Sashing Spires
(9) Stars

Fabric Requirements
- 1 yard (91.44cm) lime green for background spires
- ⅓ yard (30.45cm) purple for pies
- 2 yards dark blue for block spires, border spires,
- ½ yard (182.88cm) dark purple for stars
- ½ yard (182.88cm) light purples for stars
- 3¼ yards (297.18cm) light blue for background
- ½ yard (182.88cm) medium teal for sashing center
- ⅞ yard (80.01cm) dark teal for borders
- ½ yard (182.88cm) dark blue for binding
- (2) cuts of 1⅓ yards (121.89cm) for backing and hanging sleeve

WOF = Width of fabric

Cutting
From the lime green fabric, cut:
(96) 3" x 4" (7.62 x 10.16cm) rectangles for spires

From the purple fabric, cut:
(16) 4½" (11.43cm) squares for pies

From the dark blue fabric, cut:
(80) 2½" x 3½" 6.35 x 8.89cm) rectangles for spires
(240) 2" x 3" (5.08 x 7.62cm) rectangles
(6) 2½" x WOF strips for the binding

From the dark purple fabric, cut:
(36) 2" x 4½" (5.08 x 11.43cm) rectangles for stars

From the light purple fabric, cut:
(36) 2" x 4½" (5.08 x 11.43cm) rectangles for stars

From the light blue fabric, cut:
(16) 8" (20.32cm) squares for background
(288) 2" x 3" (5.08 x 7.62cm) rectangles for spires
(36) 2½" (6.35cm) squares cut once, diagonally, for stars
(36) 3½" (8.89cm) squares cut once, diagonally, for stars

From the medium teal fabric, cut:
(12) 2¾" x 12½" (6.99 x 31.75cm) strips

From the dark teal fabric, cut:
(2) 3½" x 42½" (8.89 x 107.95cm) strips
(2) 3½" x 48½" (8.89 x 123.19cm) strips

Star Construction
The star points are mirrored images. Use the templates on page 90 to make four dark purple points, and four light purple reversed points for each star.

1. To make a star block, lay a 2" x 4½" (5.08 x 11.43cm) dark purple rectangle, right side up on template, making sure it overlaps the sewing line by ¼" (0.64cm).

2. Align a small, light blue triangle, right side down, along the edge of the dark purple rectangle. Flip the pieces over and sew on the line. Press the piece open.

48" x 48" (121.92 x 121.92cm)
Made by Debbie Fetch, Rushville, IL
Quilted by Jodi Robinson, Enon Valley, PA

3. Repeat on the other side with the large light blue triangle. Press. Trim each piece to the outermost printed line.

Make 4 of each

4. Lay out the star pieces, with alternating dark and light purple units. Sew into squares.

5. Sew the squares into half stars and then the half stars into the whole star, pressing all the seams open. The completed star should measure 6½" (16.51cm) unfinished.

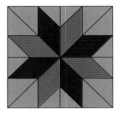

6. Referring to the directions on pages 10–19, make a total of (16) New York Beauty arcs using the dark blue 2½" x 3½" (6.35 x 8.89cm) spires, green 3" x 4" (7.62 x 10.16cm) background spires, purple 4½" (11.43cm) squares for pies and the light blue 8" squares for background.

Make 16

7. Sew (4) of the New York Beauty blocks into a square.

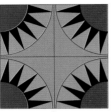

Make 4

Sashing

1. The sashing is pieced just like the New York Beauty block, only straight instead of curved. You will need (48) pieced sashing strips. (See templates, page 91.)

2. Sew (2) sashing strips together and press the seam open.

3. Sew (2) of the completed sashing sections to the 2¾" x 12½" (6.99 x 31.75cm) center strip and press the seam toward the center.

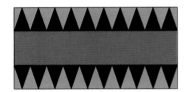

Quilt Assembly

1. Following the Quilt Assembly Diagram, lay out the blocks as shown. Sew the blocks into rows, and sew the rows to complete the quilt top. Referring to page 27, add the teal borders.

2. Layer the back, batting, and quilt top. Quilt as desired and add the binding.

Quilt Assembly Diagram

Waterlulu Mini

Have some fun! Linda made one-quarter of the quilt into a small wall hanging with bright colors. She then cut out some sea turtles from a fabric panel and fused them onto the quilt.

36" x 36" (91.44 x 91.44cm)
Made by Linda J. Hahn, Palm Bay, FL
Quilted by Jodi Robinson, Enon Valley, PA

Midtown Mambo

Midtown is the neighborhood many people picture when they think of New York. The colors in this quilt reflect the "alive and well" nightlife, and the spires create the movement of the Mambo, danced in clubs around Midtown.

Arc Foundation Requirements
(36) NYB Five Spire arcs

Fabric Requirements
- 3½ yards (320.04cm) black large print for focus fabric
- 1½ yards (137.16cm) black texture for spires
- 1 yard (91.44cm) magenta for pies and connector squares
- 2⅛ yards (194.31cm) electric blue for background spires
- 1¼ yards (114.30cm) lime green for half-square triangles
- ½ yard (45.72cm) purple for half-square triangles
- ¾ yard (68.58cm) binding fabric
- (2) cuts of 2 yards (182.88cm) each for backing and hanging sleeve

WOF = Width of fabric

Cutting
From the black large print fabric, cut:
(24) 7" (17.78cm) squares
(36) 3" (7.62cm) squares
(36) 8" (20.32cm) squares for background
(8) 6½" (16.51cm) squares

From the black texture fabric, cut:
(180) 2½" x 3½" (6.35 x 8.89cm) rectangles for spires

From the magenta fabric, cut:
(36) 4½" (11.43cm) squares for pies
(20) 3" (7.62cm) squares for connectors

From the electric blue fabric, cut:
(216) 3" x 4" (7.62 x 10.16cm) rectangles for spires

From the lime green fabric, cut:
(22) 7" (17.78cm) squares for HSTs

From the purple fabric, cut:
(10) 7" (17.78cm) squares for HSTs

From the binding fabric, cut:
(7) 2½" (6.35cm) x WOF strips

Construction
1. Following the instructions for Alternate Blocks, on page 23, make the following half-square triangle/connector square combinations using the 7" (17.78cm) squares for the HST and the 3" (7.62cm) squares for the connectors. Remember to trim the HST to 6½" (16.51cm) before adding the 3" (7.62cm) connector square.

(8) black and green HST with black connector

Make 8

(16) green and purple HST with black connector

Make 16

(12) black and purple HST with black connector

Make 12

60" x 60" (152.4 x 152.4cm)
Made by Linda J. Hahn, Palm Bay, FL
Quilted by Barbara Wolfe, Ballston Spa, NY

(20) black and green HST with magenta connector

2. Following the instructions on pages 10–19, make (36) New York Beauty five spire arcs.

Make 20

Make 36

Quilt Assembly

1. Referring to the Quilt Assembly Diagram, lay out the blocks. Sew the blocks into rows and sew the rows together to finish the quilt top.

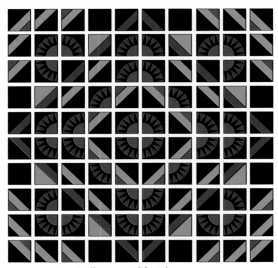

Quilt Assembly Diagram

2. Layer, baste, and quilt as desired. Add the binding. Don't forget your label!

Mambo Mini

24" (60.96cm) Square

The Mambo Mini only has two blocks. A Mini New York Beauty was made using the cutaways from the 6" New York Beauty block to make the arc foundation. We used scraps from the pink to make the 2" connector squares. We cut the rest from the extra yardage that we purchased.

To make this version, you will need to purchase an extra 1¼ yard of the large black print, ⅓ yard (30.45cm) of the lime green and ¼ yard (22.86cm) of magenta.

Don't forget, not every cutaway piece can be used for the mini. It will depend on how you cut them away from the 6" arc foundation.

HST are made using 5" (15.24cm) squares of the black print and lime green. Trim to 4½"(11.43cm). Add the 2" (5.08cm) magenta connector square to the lime green corner.

Feel free to rotate the pieces around the design wall, add more blocks, or change the orientation of the blocks to come up with your own design! We'd love to see what you come up with!

Brooklyn Blues

This project was designed using aqua, blues, and lime greens from our stash. It kind of makes us think of the Wonder Wheel ride on Coney Island, in Brooklyn.

36" (91.44 x 91.44cm) Square
Made by Linda J. Hahn, Palm Bay, FL
Quilted by Jodi Robinson, Enon Valley, PA

Arc Foundation Requirements
(8) Five Spire arc foundations

Fabric Requirements
- ½ yard (45.72cm) aqua for alternate blocks
- ¼ yard (22.86cm) lime green for spires
- 1⅓ yards (121.89cm) white for spires, alternate blocks, and inner border
- ⅝ yard (57.15cm) blue #1 for alternate blocks, pies, and outer border
- ⅓ yard (30.45cm) blue #2 for spires and center block background. This blue should contrast enough to differentiate blues in the center.
- ⅓ yard (30.45cm) for binding
- 1½ yards (137.16cm) for backing and hanging sleeve

WOF = Width of fabric

Cutting

From the aqua fabric, cut:
(4) 8" (20.32cm) squares

(4) 7" (17.78cm) squares

From the lime green fabric, cut:
(30) 2½" x 3½" (6.35 x 8.89cm) rectangles

From the white fabric, cut:
(2) 4½" X 24½" (11.43 x 62.23cm) border strips

(2) 4½" X 32½" (11.43 x 82.55cm) border strips

(4) 7" (17.78cm) squares

(48) 3" x 4" (7.62 x 10.16cm) rectangles for spires

From blue #1 fabric, cut:
(2) 2½" X 32½" (6.35 x 82.55cm) border strips

(2) 2½" x 36½" (6.35 x 92.71cm) border strips

(8) 4½" (11.43cm) squares for pies

(8) 3½" (8.89cm) squares

From blue #2 fabric, cut:
(4) 8" (20.32cm) squares

(10) 2½" x 3½" (6.35 x 8.89cm) rectangles for spires

From the binding fabric, cut:
(4) 2½" (6.35cm) x WOF strips

Construction

Make the Alternate Blocks (Make 8)

Referring to page 23, Alternate Blocks, use the 7" (17.78cm) squares of aqua and white to make 6½" (16.51cm) unfinished HSTs. Add a 3½" (8.89cm) connector square of blue #1 to the white side of the HST. After sewing, flip the connector back on itself and trim the white and blue layers from the back of the block.

Make 8

Make the New York Beauty Blocks

1. Referring to pages 10–19, make (4) NYB blocks using the 4½" (11.43cm) squares of blue #1 for the pie shape, (5) 2½" x 3½" (6.35 x 8.89cm) lime green rectangles for the spires, 3" x 4" (7.62 x 10.16cm) white rectangles for the background spires, and the 8" (11.43cm) aqua squares for the background.

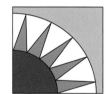

Make 4

2. Make (4) NYB blocks using the 4½" (11.43cm) squares of blue #1 for the pie shape, and the 3" x 4" (7.62 x 10.16cm) white rectangles for the background spires. Alternate the 2½" x 3½" (6.35 x 8.89cm) rectangles for the spires. Start (2) of the arcs with lime green and (2) of the arcs with blue #2.

Make 2 of each

3. Lay out the blocks in rows. Sew the blocks into rows and sew the rows to finish the quilt top.

4. Add the 4½" (11.43cm) white border, then the 2½" (6.35cm) blue border. Layer, baste, and quilt as desired. Refer to page 27, Adding Borders, for instructions.

Scarsdale Stars

A quick trip and an overnight stay in Scarsdale was far enough away from city lights to actually enjoy the night sky. This quilt shows the true colors of stars shining through wisps of nighttime clouds.

Arc Foundation Requirements

(8) 6" (15.24cm) arc foundations

(16) Mini arc foundations

Fabric Requirements

- 4¼ yards (388.62cm) dark purple for background
- (6) ⅛ yard (11.43cm) cuts or use scraps of assorted colors for stars: (2) large full sun blocks; (4) mini full sun blocks
- (2) 2 yards (182.88cm) cuts for backing and hanging sleeve
- ¾ yard (68.58cm) for binding

OPTIONAL:

- 12" (30.48cm) x WOF; about 54" (137.16cm) tulle in variety of colors: about 3 yards (274.32cm) total
- Yarns and beads for embellishing

WOF = Width of fabric

Cutting

From the dark purple fabric, cut:

(76) 6½" (16.51cm) squares for background

(8) 8" (731.52cm) squares for background

(48) 3" x 4" (7.62 x 10.16cm) rectangles for full sun background spires

(30) 2¼" x 1¾" (5.72 x 4.45cm) for mini background spires

(16) 5" (12.70cm) squares for mini background

(16) 2½" x 4½" (6.35 x 11.43cm) strips for block sashing

(16) 2½" x 6½" (6.35 x 16.51cm) for block sashing

From the assorted colors:

For EACH large full sun block, cut:

(4) 4½" (11.43cm) squares for pie

(20) 2½" x 3½" (6.35 x 8.89cm) rectangles for spires

For EACH mini full sun block, cut:

(4) 3½" (8.89cm) squares for pie

(16) 2" x 1¾" (5.08 x 4.45cm) rectangles for spires

From the binding fabric, cut:

(7) 2½" (6.35cm) x WOF strips

Construction

1. Following the instructions on pages 10–22, make (2) full sun New York Beauty blocks in two different color ways.

 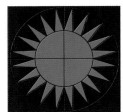

Make 2

2. Following the instructions on pages 24–25, make (4) mini full **sun** New York Beauty blocks in four different color ways.

Make 4

3. Lay out the mini blocks. Paying attention to the orientation, add a 2½" x 4½" (6.35 x 11.43cm) strip to the arc side of each block. Add a 2½" x 6½" (6.35 x 16.51cm) strip to the top of each block, again, paying attention to the orientation of the strip. Sew four arcs together to complete a block.

 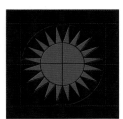

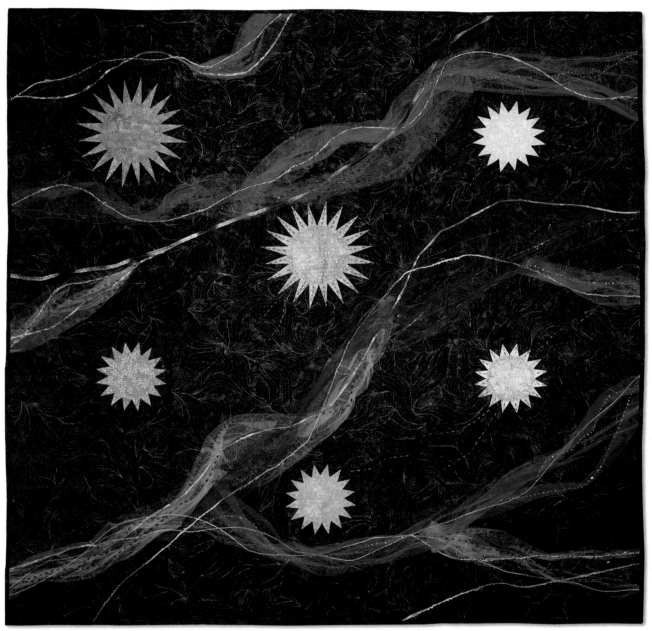

60" x 60" (152.40 x 152.40cm)
Made by Debbie Welch, Forked River, NJ
Quilted by Barbara Wolfe, Ballston Spa, NY
Embellished by Deborah G. Stanley

4. Referring to the Quilt Assembly Diagram, lay out the blocks as shown. Sew the blocks together in rows, and sew the rows together to finish the quilt top. Layer, baste and quilt as desired.

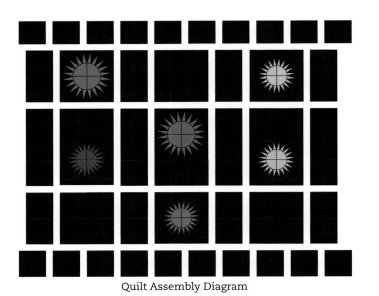

Quilt Assembly Diagram

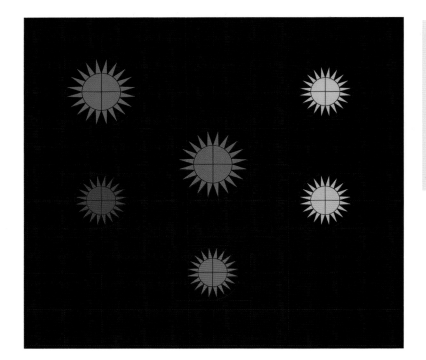

TIP

If you choose, you can add in more large or small suns, or even some half sun New York Beauty blocks. The quilt is made using a 6" (15.24cm) grid so you can easily add more stars.

Jazz It Up!

What we did:

Add swaths of tulle. We used strips approximately 12" (30.48cm) x WOF, about 54" (137.16cm) in various colors to add to the "galaxy" effect. Lay the strips in a curving line across the quilt top between the stars, pushing together for a 3D effect and changing colors as desired. Pin loosely in place. Sew down with curving lines of straight stitches near the edges of the tulle swaths to hold in place. Couch lines of yarn across the tulle and add as many lines of beads as you like. Be sure to keep any beads away from the binding seam allowance. All of the embellishments curve randomly, criss-crossing as desired. You could also add sequins, stars, and/or buttons. When you have finished adding tulle and yarn, use reserved binding strips to complete the quilt.

Dongan Hills Dingles

Dongan Hills is thought to be named so for the eastern ridge of "Todt Hill" and other areas of large hills throughout. Dingles is our name for the quiltlets, it's just kind of fun!

Arc Foundation Requirements

(36) Arc Foundations

Fabric Requirements

- 3½ yards (320.04cm) solid black for block borders
- 2¾ yards (251.46cm) lime green for spires and background
- 1½ yards (251.46cm) white for backgrounds
- ⅓ yard (30.45cm) medium bright green for pies
- ½ yard (45.72cm) reddish pink for pies
- 1 yard (91.44cm) magenta pink for backgrounds
- 1 yard (91.44cm) black and white stripe for block inner borders
- 1 yard (91.44cm) black and white dots for block connectors
- 3½ yards (320.04cm) for backing
- 3 yards (320.04cm) 90" (228.6cm) batting or queen size
- ½ yard (45.72cm) of 58"(147.32cm) wide foam interfacing

WOF = Width of fabric

Note: Foam interfacing is used to give the connecting pieces ("dingles") some substance so that the heavy quiltlets will hang straight. If you prefer, you can substitute a double layer of batting. You will need an additional ½ yard (45.72cm) of 90" (228.6cm) batting.

Cutting

From the black solid fabric, cut:
(9) 18" (45.72cm) squares for block quiltlets
(100) 2½" x 3½" (6.35 x 8.89cm) rectangles for spires

From the lime green fabric, cut:
(20) 8" (20.32cm) squares for background and spires
(120) 3" x 4" (7.62 x 10.16cm) rectangles for spires
(80) 2½" x 3½" (6.35 x 8.89cm) rectangles for spires

From the white fabric, cut:
(16) 8" (20.32cm) squares for background
(6) 2½" (6.35cm) x WOF strips for block binding

From the medium bright green fabric, cut:
(16) 4½" (11.43cm) squares for pies

From the reddish pink fabric, cut:
(20) 4½" (11.43cm) squares for pies

From the magenta pink fabric, cut:
(96) 3" x 4" (7.62 x 10.16cm) rectangles for spires

From the black and white stripe fabric, cut:
(8) 2½" (6.35cm) x WOF strips for block binding

From the black and white dot fabric, cut:
(24) 6½" (16.51cm) squares for quiltlet connectors

From the backing fabric, cut:
(9) 18" (45.72cm) squares for quiltlet backing
(9) 14" (35.56cm) squares for block backing

From the batting, cut:
(Larger quiltlets use a double layer of batting to add weight to the squares.) These squares could be cut from a queen size or 3 yards of 90" batting.

(18) 18" (45.72cm) squares for quiltlet blocks
(9) 14" (35.56cm) squares for blocks

From the foam interfacing cut:
(12) 6½" (16.51cm) squares of foam interfacing OR
(24) 6½" (16.51cm) squares for double batting for connectors

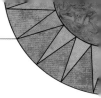

57" x 57" (144.78 x 144.78cm)
Made by Linda J. Hahn and Deborah G. Stanley
Quilted by Linda J. Hahn

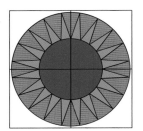

Construction

1. Following the instructions on pages 10–22, make the following full sun New York Blocks.

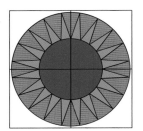

Make 4
white background, bright green pies, lime green spires, and magenta background spires.

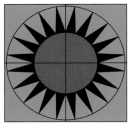

Make 5
lime green background, reddish pink pies, black spires and lime green background spires.

2. Quilt each of these full sun blocks individually using one layer of batting and 14" (35.56cm) backing. Trim to 12½" (31.75cm).

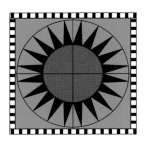

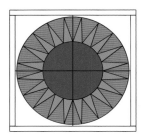

3. Bind using white binding for white background blocks and black/white stripe binding for lime green background blocks.

4. Using 18" (45.72cm) black squares, 18" (45.72cm) backing squares and (2) layers of batting, construct and quilt (9) larger quiltlets. Any allover design will work but only the outer few inches will be visible. Trim each to a 16" (40.64cm) square.

5. Center a completed and bound full sun New York Beauty block on a quiltlet. Stitch in the ditch between the binding and the New York Beauty block to secure block.

6. Bind each quiltlet with black binding, adding the hanging sleeves (if using) to two of the lime green blocks and one white block.

7. Layer foam interfacing (or double batting), and (2) 6½" (16.51cm) black and white dot squares right sides together. Sew ¼" (0.64cm) from edges, leaving a 3" (7.62cm) opening on one side for turning. Clip corners, turn and close opening using a hand or machine stitch. Quilt the connector dingle using a grid or any allover design. Repeat to make (12) connector dingles.

Assemble the Quilt

1. Pin the connector "dingle" in place behind the first quiltlet, centering top to bottom, and overlapping ¾" (1.91cm) on the back of the quiltlet. Stitch in the ditch between the binding and the edge of the quiltlet to secure the dingle, backstitching at the beginning and end. Attach the additional quiltlets and connectors in the same manner to finish the first row.

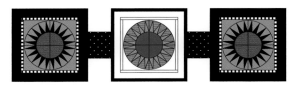

2. Add connector dingles to the bottom of each of the quiltlets in the first row, centering side to side with ¾" (1.91cm) overlap on the back.

3. Repeat the steps to add the second and third rows of quiltlets and connectors to finish the quilt.

Optional: The easiest way to hang this quilt is using individual hanging sleeves on the top three quiltlets and a decorative curtain pole. If you wish to hang the quilt using hanging sleeves, you will need ⅝ yard (57.15cm) additional backing fabric or fabric of your choice for (3) hanging sleeves each measuring about 14" (35.56cm) long.

Cayuga Coral

Named after the indigenous Cayuga people, this historic little village sits on Cayuga Lake. It's in north-central New York, close to Lake Ontario, and a favorite destination to find some quiet from city noise.

Arc Foundation Requirements
(40) Five Spire arc foundations

Fabric Requirements
- 2¾ yards (251.46cm) light peach for background and half-square triangles
- 2½ yards (228.6cm) dark peach for background and half-square triangles
- 1½ yards (137.16cm) red for spires
- 2⅜ yards (217.17cm) cream for spires
- 1 yard (91.44cm) gold for pies and background
- 4 yards (320.04cm) for backing and hanging sleeve
- ⅝ yard (57.15cm) red for binding

WOF = Width of fabric

Cutting
From the light peach fabric, cut:
(28) 6½" (16.51cm) squares

(16) 7½" (19.05cm) squares

(8) 8" (20.32cm) squares for background

(4) 9" (22.86cm) squares for HST New York Beauty background

From the dark peach fabric, cut:
(16) 7½" (19.05cm) squares

(20) 8" (20.32cm) squares for background

(4) 9" (22.86cm) squares for HST New York Beauty background

(4) 4½" (11.43cm) squares

(8) 5" (11.43cm) squares for HST for split pie

From the red fabric, cut:
(200) 2½" x 3½" (6.35 x 8.89cm) rectangles for spires

(7) 2½" (6.35cm) strips for binding

From the cream fabric, cut:
(240) 3" x 4" (7.62 x 10.16cm) rectangles

From the gold fabric, cut:
(20) 4½" (11.43cm) squares

(4) 8" (20.32cm) squares for background

(8) 5" (12.7cm) squares for HST split pie

Construction
1. Following the instructions for Alternate Blocks, on page 23, use the 7½" (20.32cm) squares of light peach and dark peach to make a total of (32) half-square triangles. Trim to 6½" (16.51cm).

Make 32

2. Follow the instructions on pages 10–19w, to make the following five-spire arc color combinations:

Make 4
dark peach background and a gold pie

Make 4
gold background and a dark peach pie

Make 8
light peach background and a gold pie

3. Use the 9" (22.86cm) light peach and dark peach squares and the 5" (12.7cm) dark peach and gold squares to make half-square triangles. Do not trim.

60" x 60" (152.40 x 152.40cm)
Made by Rebecca Szabo, Howell, NJ
Quilted by Barbara Wolfe, Ballston Spa, NY
Embellishments by Roxanne Kermidas, Palm Bay, FL

4. Use the half-square triangles from step 3 to make the following arc foundations with split pies and split backgrounds.

Make 8
dark peach split pie
on the left, and a dark
peach background

Make 8
dark peach split pie
on the right, and a dark
peach background

Make 4
dark peach split
background on the
right, and a gold pie.

Make 4
dark peach split
background on the left,
and a gold pie

Assembly

1. Referring to the Quilt Assembly Diagram, lay out the blocks in rows and sew together to make the rows. Sew the rows together to complete the quilt top.

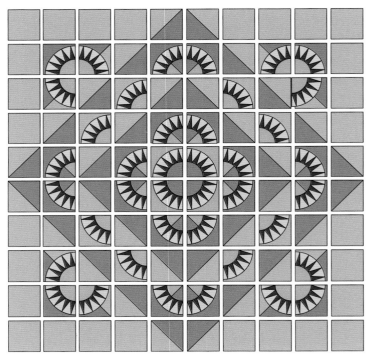

Quilt Assembly Diagram

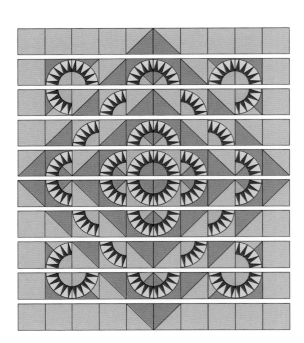

2. Layer, baste, and quilt as desired! Don't forget the label.

TIP

You can arrange the blocks in any number of ways. Feel free to create your own design!

Jazz It Up!

What we did:
We used a crystal applicator to add hot-fix crystals for a little sparkle.

Other ideas:
You could also add some bugle beads or sparkly seed beads. The large, open space arcs are a great place to showcase custom quilting.

Arc Foundation Templates

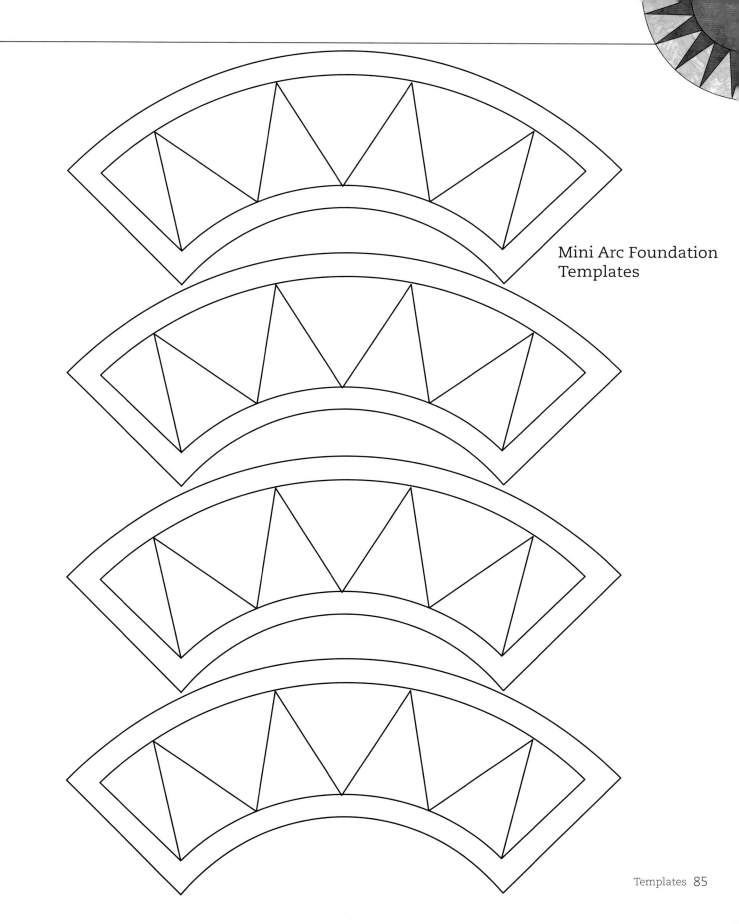

Mini Arc Foundation
Templates

Mini Pie, Background and
Spire Templates

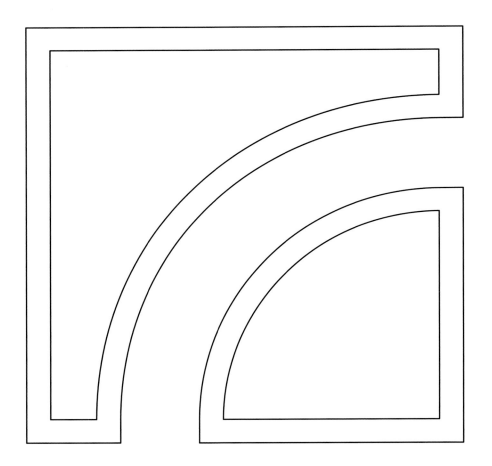

Pie and Background
Templates

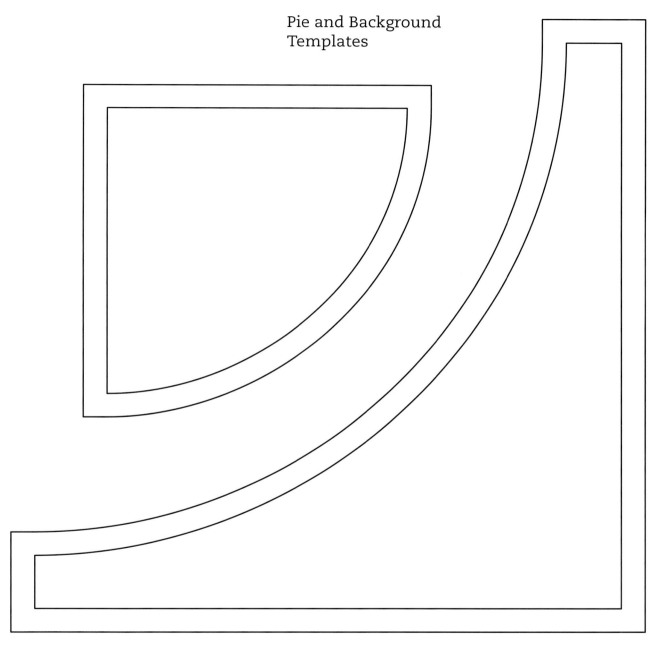

Waterlily Templates

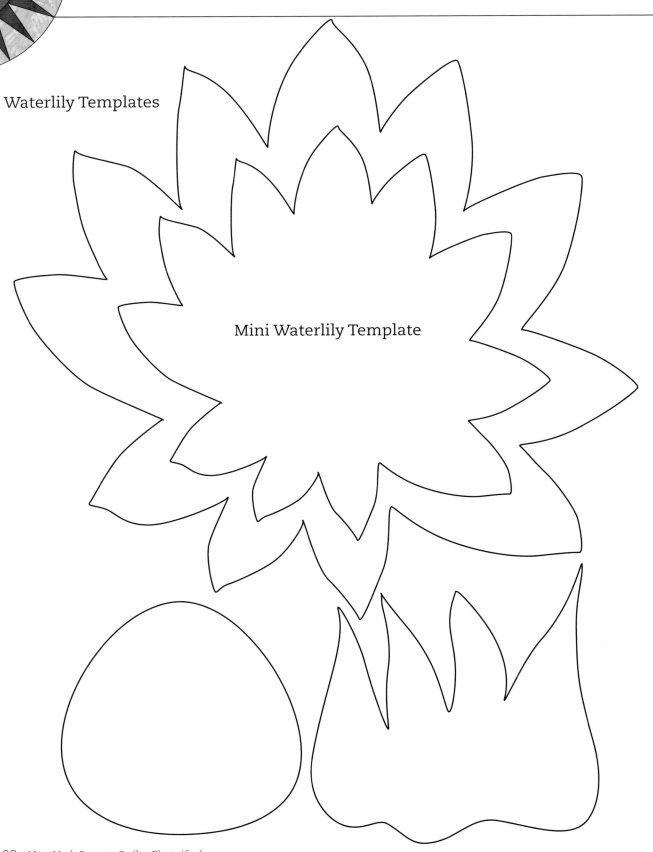

Mini Waterlily Template

Mini Waterlily Templates

Split Spire Template

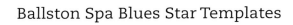

Ballston Spa Blues Star Templates

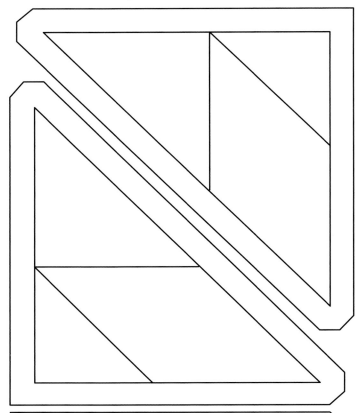

Cut 1 and 1 Reverse

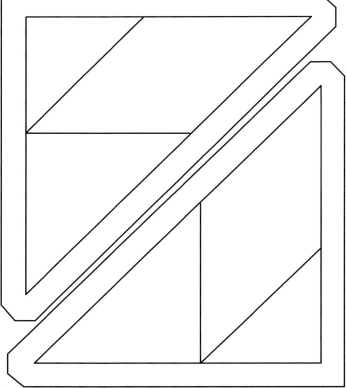

Ballston Spa Blues Border Templates

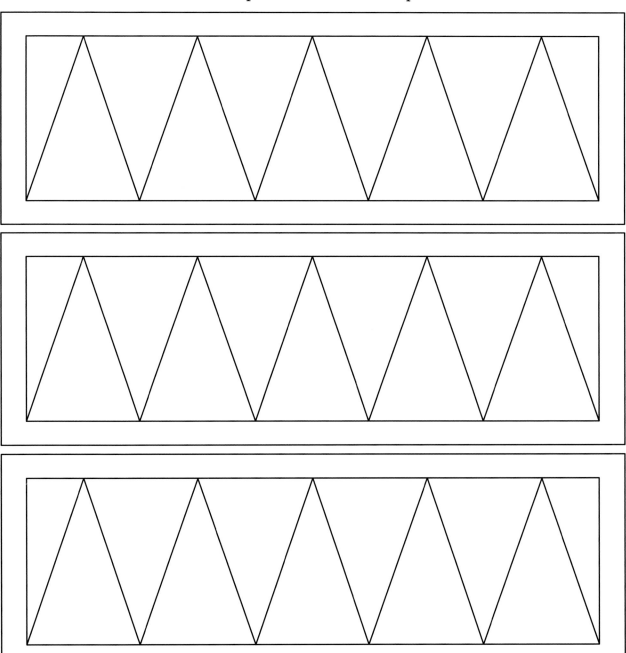

Inspiration Gallery

Liberty Lace

Made by Deborah G. Stanley

This quilt was our inspiration to empty a box of dainty lace treasures. Lace doilies center the New York Beauty blocks and an antique button centers each doily. Lengths of lace were sewn to the borders. We love being able to look at these beauties with treasures from the past.

Inspiration Gallery

Palmyra Prowler

Made by Linda J. Hahn

I was the "prowler" around the historic village of Palmyra, New York. But I thought it better to put this beautiful cat in the quilt, prowling around the woods of Palmyra! Be creative!

About the Authors

The Collaboration

Deborah and Linda have been "besties" for over 20 years. You may have seen them walking around the quilt show floor together. They enjoy traveling to different quilt show venues and taking classes together, although at times, there have been some disagreements over whether the temperature in the room should be set at "chilly" or "arctic." They have collaborated on many magazine and fabric company designs, as well as their own patterns. They are very successful at bouncing ideas and opinions off each other.

Despite now being separated by miles, they speak to each other on the phone daily and arrange to meet for play or work dates.

Photo by: Bonnie McCaffery

Linda and Deb are available for lectures and workshops, please contact: *www.froghollowdesigns.com*

Dedications

Linda

This book is dedicated to my beloved sister, Susan Stillinger, who passed away suddenly on April 30, 2016. We were so happy to finally be living close to each other again…so many plans…that were not to be.

Not a day goes by that I do not think of you—I miss you so very, very much.

Susan June Stillinger
June 30, 1949–April 30, 2016

Deborah

This book is dedicated to my husband, Steve, who has always supported me in all of my endeavors. Although he doesn't always understand why I am so excited about fabric and thread and beads and yarn, he always manages to convey enthusiasm about the results. Also, I would not be where I am today without my mother, Alice Gillen, who taught me to sew doll clothes on the same Necchi sewing machine that she used to make my baby clothes—I wish she could see this book completed.

Acknowledgments

We would like to thank our fabulous piecing team, Nancy Rock, Janet Byard, Rebecca Szabo, Debbie Welch, Debbie Fetch and Roxanne Kermidas for helping us make quilts for this book!

A special thank you to Bill Volckening for writing the Foreword.

Thank you to our awesome machine quilters, Jodi Robinson and Barbara Wolfe.

We also would like to thank Hoffman California Fabrics, Timeless Treasures Fabrics, Aurifil Thread and Fairfield Processing for providing some of the fabulous fabrics, thread and batting for our projects!

Thank you to Deb and Jim Welch and Rob and Judy Engime for your many years of support and encouragement.

Finally, a big thank you to Laurel Albright, Sue Voegtlin and the entire team at Fox Chapel Publishing for bringing our ideas to life! We are so thrilled to be a part of the Fox Chapel team!

DEBORAH G. STANLEY is an independent designer, whose work has been published in many magazines, including *Quilt* magazine, *Love of Quilting, Modern Patchwork, American Quilter* and *Quilter's World*. She has designed consumer projects for several fabric companies, including Northcott, RJR, and Elizabeth's Studio. Her specialty is simple, easy-to-complete sewing and quilting projects, especially lap quilts and handbags. Using embellishments to "kick up" quilts is her favorite way to add personality. Her work has appeared in several of Linda Hahn's books, and her quilt "Five O'Clock Somewhere" was the cover quilt for Linda's book *Rock That Quilt Block: Hourglass* (AQS 2016).

Deb lives in New Jersey with her husband, Steve, and Frodo, a very spoiled cat. When not quilting, she enjoys reading and crafts of all kinds, as well as practicing her newly acquired long arm skills.

Photo by: Bonnie McCaffery

LINDA J. HAHN is a multiple award-winning author, fabric designer, pattern designer, long arm quilter, and sought-after speaker. Her books *New York Beauty Simplified* (AQS 2011) and *New York Beauty Diversified* (AQS 2013) won Bronze and Gold medals respectively in the Independent Publishers Living Now Book Awards. She has three other books, two of which have also won awards. Linda is thrilled to have her first batik fabric collection released in 2019 from Northcott Silk. Her work has been featured in many of your favorite quilting magazines. She was named the 2009 National Quilting Association Certified Teacher of the Year.

Linda recently moved to Palm Bay, Florida, where she lives with her husband, Allan. When not quilting, she can be found reading CIA/Black Ops novels while floating in her pool. She is a licensed Zumba instructor and also holds many specialty Zumba licenses. Linda is available to visit with your guild, group or retreat. Visit her website at *www.froghollowdesigns.com* for more information.

Photo by: Bonnie McCaffery

Resources

Foundation Paper, Stencils, Kits
www.froghollowdesigns.com

Thread
Aurifil
www.aurifil.com

Fabrics
Hoffman California
www.hoffmancaliforniafabrics.com

Timeless Treasures
www.ttfabrics.com

Batting
Nature-Fil
Fairfield Processing Company
www.fairfieldworld.com

Fusible Web
The Warm Company
www.warmcompany.com

Embellishments
Yarns, beads, tulle, Angelina fibers,
silk flowers, charms, buttons, wiggle eyes,
embroidery floss:
Your local craft store, specialty bead store,
local yarn shop or your knitting neighbor

Long Arm Quilters
Jodie Robinson
www.jrdesigns.wordpress.com

Barbara Wolfe
A Winding Thread Quilting
awindingthread@gmail.com
515-884-9923

Bill Volckening
New York Beauty
Quilts from the Volckening Collection

www.quiltmania.com

To schedule a visit with Linda for your guild,
group or retreat, please contact:

Linda J. Hahn
Lawnquilt@aol.com
3321-586-4005
www.froghollowdesigns.com